Tejano Empire

NUMBER SEVEN:
The Clayton Wheat Williams
Texas Life Series

Tejano Empire

Life on the South Texas Ranchos

ANDRÉS TIJERINA

Illustrations by Ricardo M. Beasley
Detail drawings by Servando G. Hinojosa

TEXAS A&M UNIVERSITY PRESS
College Station

Tejano brands by
Servando G. Hinojosa

The paper used in this book meets
the minimum requirements
of the American National Standard
for Permanence of Paper
for Printed Library Materials, z39.48-1984.
Binding materials have been chosen
for durability.

Library of Congress Cataloging-in-Publication Data

Tijerina, Andrés.
    Tejano empire : life on the south Texas ranchos /
Andrés Tijerina ; illustrations by Ricardo M. Beasley;
detail drawings by Servando G. Hinojosa. — 1st ed.
        p.   cm. — (The Clayton Wheat Williams Texas
life series; no. 7)
        Includes bibliographical references (p.) and index
        ISBN 0-89096-834-9 (alk.paper)
            1. Mexican Americans — Texas — Nueces River
    Valley — Social life and customs.   2. Ranch life —
    Texas — Nueces River Valley.   3. Nueces River
    Valley (Tex.) — Social life and customs.
        I. Title.   II. Series.
F392.N82T55   1998
976.4'110046872073—DC21   98-20980
                                                                        CIP

ISBN 13: 978-1-60344-051-6 (pbk.)
ISBN 10: 1-60344-051-8 (pbk.)

In the spirit of my *suegros*

Ramón and Amelia García

OF SAN DIEGO, TEXAS

CONTENTS

ILLUSTRATIONS

In March of 1995, the death of Tejano music's brightest star, Selena, at the hands of a jealous fan attracted national attention. Unfortunately, it was the first time the Corpus Christi native gained truly national attention, the first time her name was mentioned on the three major television networks. Most Americans had never even heard of Tejano music, the Texas-Mexican counterpart to Nashville country music. News reporters were surprised by the number of mourners who attended her wake, and wondered how such a commanding icon for the Hispanic community could have almost completely escaped the attention of the non-Tejano world.

Selena's death brought national attention not only to the tragic death of a young woman, but also to her music, which reflected her South Texas roots. Modern Tejano music, however, was not the first musical trend to emerge from the region. In the early 1920s, South Texas Hispanics had developed a highly stylized music genre called *conjunto,* a peculiar combination of guitars and accordions that captured the musical tastes of Hispanics across the nation for several decades.

Clearly there was a vast cultural gap between Tejanos and non-Tejanos, between the Anglo perception of Mexican Americans and the hidden Mexican-American reality that the Anglo does not see. The reality is that Tejanos have traditionally played important leadership roles in the larger Hispanic culture of the United States. For example, a 1911 Tejano conference on social justice was clearly a precursor to later Hispanic social movements. The conference, which convened in Laredo and was called *El Congreso Mejicanista* (the Mexicanist Congress), represented the collective action of some of the most dynamic leaders in South Texas. Tejanos were largely a rural people, but they had been in South Texas longer than any Anglos, and their leaders saw the importance of articulating their needs in a changing world. A few years later, many of these same South Texas leaders met again in Corpus Christi, in coalition with other groups, to form the League of United Latin American Citizens, or LULAC—the nation's largest Hispanic civil rights organization. And in 1947, South Texas Hispanic leaders met again in Corpus Christi to organize the American G.I. Forum, which advocated for Hispanic veterans' rights after World War II. Together, these leaders and these organizations provided much of the foundation for the Chicano social movement that emerged in the 1960s.

More then a century earlier, Tejanos had already made a major contribution to the American industries of cattle, sheep, goat raising, and mustanging—all of which originated in South Texas between San Antonio, Corpus Christi, Brownsville, and Laredo. This region, the Tejanos' nineteenth-century homeland, produced Tejano leaders and initiatives that influenced not only South Texas, and not only Hispanics, but the rest of the nation. The special qualities that enabled these South Texans to play this dynamic role pose one of the major inquiries of this book.

To understand what led to the unique Tejano leadership initiatives of the twentieth century, one must first understand the Tejano ranch community in the period between 1836 and 1886. For it is this community that provided Tejanos with their essential culture—their strong family values, cultural loyalty, and networks of communication, as well as their shared reaction to Anglo-American in-migration. One pillar of the Tejano community was the ranch family, which preserved and transmitted Tejano history, language, and culture from one generation to the next and from family to family through the network of *compadre* linkages. Ultimately, the family provided stability during the many traumatic events in nineteenth-century Texas. For example, as Anglos and European immigrants began to arrive in South Texas, imposing a government that seemed to deny Tejanos a positive role in American society, many Tejanos turned inward, toward their ranch families, for strength in the face of change.

Unable to count on support from their Anglo-dominated government, Tejanos relied on the ranch family, with its strong group cohesiveness and its network of communities, to preserve their own cultural identity. Indeed, many twentieth-century sociologists have marveled at the tenacious cultural and language loyalties that have distinguished Tejanos from other ethnic minorities in Texas and the United States.

The Tejano leaders who formed the important twentieth-century Tejano organizations—including Eduardo Idar of Laredo, Ben Garza of Corpus Christi, Alonso Perales of Alice, J. T. Canales of Falfurrias, and a host of others—were all descendants of the nineteenth-century ranch families of South Texas. They called themselves Latin Americans by 1920, but most of them had been born on ranches or in Tejano ranch towns. By 1927, Latin Americans began to assert their way into American society—into grand juries, school boards, and the state legislature. Their organizational efforts began to enter the pages of Texas history, as indicated by such seminal studies as Mario T.

García's *Mexican Americans: Leadership, Ideology, & Identity, 1930–1960* (New Haven: Yale University Press, 1989) and Juan Gómez-Quiñones' *Roots of Chicano Politics, 1600–1940* (Albuquerque: University of New Mexico Press, 1994).

Ironically, however, the preceding generations on the Tejano ranches have almost completely escaped the attention of historians. A few studies have reviewed the social and cultural aspects of Tejanos in South Texas, such as Joe S. Graham's *El Rancho in South Texas* (Denton: University of North Texas Press, 1994) and Arnoldo DeLeón's *The Tejano Community, 1836–1900* (Albuquerque: University of New Mexico Press, 1982). But even these works have only peripherally explained the cultural roots of these early twentieth-century Tejano leaders.

One reason for the limited number of historical studies specifically addressing the Tejano ranches between 1836 and 1886 is the lack of formal documentation and writings by Tejanos of that period. Few Tejanos served as government officials during those years, so they left no judicial reports, policy statements, or historic speeches. Few of them participated in political conventions, so their political views were not recorded in the archives. Only a few Tejanos were recorded in police or military reports, and most of them were considered bandits by the Anglo-dominated officer corps. Another reason, of course, is that most writers of Texas history have not understood or have cared little about the Tejano point of view.

A few writers have dedicated themselves to preserving Tejano ranch history. One of these was Fermina Guerra, whose unpublished master's thesis, "Mexican and Spanish Folklore and Incidents in Southwest Texas," lamented that the story of the Tejano rancheros was "lost forever." Fortunately, it is not, because Guerra did not let that happen. Her 1941 thesis from the University of Texas, now in the Lorenzo de Zavala State Library archives at the capitol in Austin, is a starting point for the history that is reconstructed in this book. Another classic work is the master's thesis of Jovita González, who wrote "Social Life in Cameron, Starr, and Zapata Counties" at the University of Texas at Austin in 1930. A third work, *Ranch Life in Hidalgo County after 1850,* was by a schoolteacher, Emilia Schunior Ramirez. Roberto M. Villareal, who had a master's in nuclear physics and a second master's in history, wrote his thesis on "The Mexican-American Vaqueros of the Kenedy Ranch: A Social History." All of these writers were proud descendants of Tejano ranch families, and their pioneering histories have provided the pieces of a historical puzzle that can and must be fitted together. But first, the pieces must be organized into a pattern or a conceptual framework.

This study of early Tejano history has been developed from different sources than the traditional archives and official documents, because traditional records were not always available for Tejanos in this time period. The historical base for this book has been established through numerous anecdotes from unpublished materials, including the works of Guerra, González, Ramirez, and Villareal. Then the historical setting for these stories has been examined in the material culture that Tejano families left behind—that is, their old houses, their tools, and their artifacts. These material objects have then been compared to the official records from government censuses and land titles. In order to verify and reinforce the book's non-standard sources, I have applied a triangulation of source information for my documentation. For example, an event may be documented from three perspectives, such as a contemporary traveler's account, an unpublished account of contemporary folklore, and demographic or physical evidence from official records. This three-way documentation may offer some reassurance to the reader and to the author that these facts provide a truthful historical construct of the Tejano ranch community.

The conceptual framework or paradigm for analyzing the essential elements of the Tejano ranch community adapts what James C. Scott described as a "hidden transcript" in his book *Domination and the Arts of Resistance: Hidden Transcripts* (New Haven: Yale University Press, 1990). Scott's paradigm provides a means for studying the history of groups who have been isolated and dominated by some other group—as happened to Tejanos after 1836, when Anglo-American immigration began to overwhelm them politically and economically. Before that year, Tejano life was recorded in a rich collection of documents known as the Béxar Archives. But as Tejanos became a minority or subordinate group, overwhelmed numerically and politically by Anglo-Americans, they generated a wholly different set of historical records and sources. Often subordinated in power relationships with their new Anglo-American neighbors, Tejanos went underground or moved onto the remote ranches, taking their literary record with them and thus complicating the paper trail for the modern historical researcher.

However, by using nonstandard historical sources and a paradigm like Scott's, a historical work can nonetheless construct a clear picture of the Tejano ranch community in the nineteenth century. Scott has argued that a valid historical record may be found in poetry, songs, rhymes, ballads, and old stories. Thus, even folklore may be combined with material evidence and official records to provide insights into the essential elements of the Tejano ranch community. A historian might even begin to understand the formula for action within the Tejano community; that is, the spark that incited Tejanos to protest, the motivation that compelled them to organize, and the goals that guided them. Another historical researcher, Ranajit Guha, has argued in *Elementary Aspects of Peasant Insurgency in Colonial India* (Delhi: Oxford University Press, 1983) that rural families could have conscious leaders, economic planning, political objectives, and group consciousness—qualities that apply to Tejanos as well. They may not have been invited to attend the political conventions of the 1860s, but they had their own informal circles where they discussed political matters. They were not government officials, but they had a patriarchal council of ranch leaders. And their interfamilial linkages served as critical networks to preserve not only their heritage, but their power base in their lands and their cattle. A reconstructed history, then, might present not only a clear picture of Tejano ranch life, but also an understanding of the ideas within that community.

Throughout the nineteenth century, Tejano families and their leaders were defining a set of values and an elaborate Tejano idealogy, establishing the ideals and goals that LULAC and the G.I. Forum eventually acted upon in the twentieth century. Tejano values and the Tejano dream were also reflected in the music of the ill-fated singer, Selena.

Just like Martin Luther King, Jr., who finally enunciated his dream in 1963, Tejanos had been defining their goals and the aspirations of their community. King did not simply "make it up" on the spur of the moment in Washington, D.C., when he told an assembled crowd that "I have a dream." He had learned it from elders in the African-American church and from African-American families who had been preserving those dreams since the days of slavery in the Old South. The Negro spirituals, the Br'er Rabbit tales, and cultural artifacts all preserved the dream for one of their sons, someday, to tell it to the world. The Tejano dream is in the works of Jovita González, Fermina Guerra, and Roberto Villareal, to be sure. But it is also in the words of the Tejano ballads about Gregorio Cortez and Juan "Cheno" Cortina. It is in the nineteenth-century homes made of *sillar* stone, many of which still stand throughout South Texas.

There is a silent story in the stone chimneys that were used to prepare the Tejano ranch meals, and in the rifle portholes in the walls that served to protect the family. And finally, the Tejano dream is reflected in the twentieth-century teenagers who saw in Selena an innocent, beautiful, loving role model. Although Selena probably never read a history of the Tejano ranch families, she vividly displayed their pride, their cultural values, their racial features, as well as their musical heritage.

This book attempts to provide a unified historical account of rural Tejano life and culture in the nineteenth century. It also attempts to explain why and how that culture could have been distorted or omitted from the pages of Texas history for so long, and to provide a viable paradigm for accessing previously untapped historical sources among seemingly inarticulate groups. My purpose is not to write a complete history of Hispanics in Texas during the nineteenth century, either geographically or topically. The book makes no attempt to chronicle all of the major events in that period, to cover all the Hispanic Texans in the trans-Pecos region, to describe urban Tejano life, or to include the pockets of original Tejanos in isolated regions like Nacogdoches. The book focuses on the growing population base of Tejanos in South Texas and its cultural nexus to northern Mexico, especially in the period between the Texas Revolution and 1886.

The book deals little with the period after 1886, when Tejano ranch society experienced major demographic changes. As other Mexicans from Mexico moved into towns after 1880, they overwhelmed the native Tejano community, the majority of whom lived in the region of Texas south of the San Antonio River, east of Laredo's Webb County, and along the Gulf Coast south to the Rio Grande. The term Tejano is used to facilitate the reader's understanding of the subject group, but it does not accurately apply to all Hispanics in Texas because of changing national boundaries. Indeed, the greater number of persons identified herein as Tejanos did not consider themselves Americans or Texas citizens until 1848, when the Treaty of Guadalupe Hidalgo resolved the dispute over the region between the Nueces River and the Rio Grande. Most of them referred to themselves as Mexicanos or as Mexico-Tejanos during the subject period. But they were in fact, related by bloodlines and by culture to the pre-1836 Tejanos of San Antonio de Béxar and Goliad. And for these Mexico-Tejanos, the shortened term Tejano most clearly defines the cultural continuity between the original Tejanos and the twentieth-century Mexican Americans of Texas.

This book must acknowledge the valuable contributions of early historians such as Jovita González and Fermina Guerra, who personally interviewed the last surviving Tejanos after the turn of the century. In 1929, Jovita González interviewed Don Francisco Guerra y Guerra, descendant of Don Francisco Guerra, surveyor of the Mier land grants in 1768; Guerra y Guerra turned ninety-eight the year she interviewed him. That year she also interviewed Doña Isabel Garcia of San Diego; Doña Domasita Cisneros de Canales, a direct descendant of Juan Nepomuceno Cortina; and Mrs. Dolores Guerra de Treviño. Mrs. Treviño, who was sixty-five in 1929, had "witnessed many dances of St. John's celebrations at her father's ranch, Las Viboras, in Starr County." González's and Guerra's master's theses could claim all of the value of many published works, and under other circumstances, Roberto Villareal's thesis might today be a published history book. Recently, the work of my own colleague, Joe S. Graham, in *El Rancho in South Texas* and of his student, Mary

Anna Casstevens, in her intensive study of the Randado Ranch, have contributed significant documentation as well.

I must express profound gratitude to the heirs of the R. M. Beasley estate for allowing me the honor of publishing the art of Ricardo M. Beasley for the first time. Rick Garcia and Connie Beasley were so giving of their time and generosity in making the R. M. Beasley Art Collection available for this book, and Grace Reyes was also generous with her time and hospitality in making the materials available to me. Beasley was an artist of the San Diego, Texas area, who devoted his life to capturing the spirit of the *vaquero* throughout Duval County and neighboring counties. He was born in South Texas in 1908 and did most of his art in the early twentieth century. It took me months of research to find his art collection and to arrange for its publication in this book, particularly because he wanted his art to speak for itself and for him. I firmly believe that his spirit has found its own dear message in my story of Tejano pioneers on the ranching frontier.

I must also thank Servando G. Hinojosa for his wonderful detailed drawings of scenes from South Texas ranch life. His valuable contribution will always be appreciated.

While teaching at Texas A&M University-Kingsville in South Texas, I had the rare opportunity in my classes to teach Texas history to the direct descendants of the Tejano ranch families. My students were hearing for the first time a formal history of their own families. Also, my wife, Juanita, is a direct descendant of the Solís family, who had a typical Tejano ranch, El Rancho Solís in Duval County. I was fascinated when her father told ranch stories, and her uncles took me to the actual nineteenth-century homes of their ranch ancestors and to a ranch *taconaso* dance deep, deep in the chaparral. I never expected that I would someday write a history of their ranches. I was fortunate to become a member of such a family. And my fondest dream would be to give to the reader a sense of the deep commitment that these Tejanos had for their family and their community in daily life.

Andrés Tijerina
AUSTIN

INTRODUCTION

There exists in Texas a common tendency among Anglo-Americans, particularly among Americans of one or two generations' stay in the country, to look down upon the Mexicans of the border counties as interlopers, undesirable aliens, and a menace to the community. Those among the last group named who have this opinion should before making a definite stand consider the following: First, that the majority of these so-called undesirable aliens have been in the state long before Texas was Texas; second, that these people were here long before these new Americans crowded the deck of the immigrant ship; third, that a great number of the Mexican people in the border did not come as immigrants, but are the descendants of the agraciados *who held grants from the Spanish crown.*

—Jovita González, 1930

South Texas was first settled in the mid-1700s by Spanish and Mexican families who entered the region under the leadership of José de Escandon. A wealthy Spanish count, Escandon brought the pioneering families to establish their ranches in South Texas. At that time the region was part of the northern Mexican province of Nuevo Santander, which stretched from the Nueces River and along the Gulf Coast south to Tampico. The early Spanish explorers referred to this section of the Mexican coast as El Seno Mexicano. Mexico itself was still a colony called *Nueva España* or New Spain, and would remain under Spanish rule until 1821.

The Spanish colonial administrators had originally intended for Texas and

Nuevo Santander to protect the northern line of New Spain. Their word for this protective line of defense was *frontera,* and their strategy was to settle the *frontera* with a hearty stock of people who would serve as a buffer colony protecting Monterrey and Saltillo from the hostile American Indians of Texas. Thus, in their very origins, the ranch communities along the Lower Rio Grande developed a distinctive identity, noticeably different from the people of interior Mexico. The settlers of the Escandon *frontera* came with weapons to protect their neighbors to the south, and with a sense of duty that began to distinguish them from other Spaniards immediately as they settled on the harsh *frontera.* It also distinguished them from the Anglo-American settlers who later came westward into Texas. Anglo Americans thought of South Texas as a "frontier," a virgin area open to exploration and settlement. The Spanish word *frontera,* however, means "border," a defensive line, closed to penetration. The ranch families along the Rio Grande were there to protect the *frontera* from Anglos and from hostile Indians alike.

The Spaniards had fought centuries of medieval warfare against the Moors in Spain, and in the 1500s, after Columbus discovered the New World, they fought against civilizations like the Aztecs and Incas as well. Wherever they conquered, they had become accustomed to establishing a defensive line, or *frontera,* designed as a unified system of fortified towns, missions, forts, and ranches.

A fortified town on the Spanish *frontera* was called a municipality. Its purpose was more than simply to house settlers. The municipality was a defensive settlement with jurisdiction over the surrounding territory for several miles around. As such, it was rather like a combination of an American city and county in one. The municipality of Mier, for example, which Escandon established on the Rio Grande, held jurisdiction over the distant ranches as far north as present-day San Diego, Texas.

The Spanish municipalities were usually laid in a line that formed the *frontera.* Beyond those municipalities lay a defensive band of sparsely populated lands stretching up to two hundred miles. The depopulated land, referred to as the *despoblado,* was considered an integral part of the home municipality. Although the residents of the *despoblado* might be many miles from the cities of the border, they fulfilled a vital mission, defending their relatives in the home municipality and providing it with beef and ranch products. They also depended on the municipality for trade and for the legal status of their land grants.

The South Texas *frontera* differed in some respects from the standard Spanish *frontera* structure used in other parts of the Spanish world. For example, Escandon did not make extensive use of the customary missions or the garrisoned forts called presidios to protect his municipalities. He depended instead on a wide band of ranches for defense as well as for food supplies. Thus, he placed his towns on the south bank of the Rio Grande river and laid his first ranches in a solid line of land grants along the river's north bank. The fertile north bank would later be advertised under the government of the United States of America as "The Magic Valley."

The ranches that bordered the river were laid out in elongated rectangles, with a narrow front on the riverbank and two long sides leading northward from the river, sometimes stretching up to twenty miles north. By giving each rancher a narrow front on the Rio Grande, Escandon allowed for a greater number of them to use the river's life-giving waters. And by extending the length of the land grants, he provided each with the required acreage of at least 4,000 acres. Such an elongated rectangle was called a *porción* because each rancher had a "portion" of the river's water. Located on the fertile river delta, the *porciónes* were capable of producing farm crops as well as ranch livestock. These original *porciónes* quickly became the symbol of social rank not only to the original pioneers, but also to their descendants in the twentieth century.

Beyond the first tier of *porciónes,* Escandon established a wider band of large cattle-grazing ranches. These were scattered over roughly the next 200 miles into the *despoblado* to the north—the country between the Rio Grande and the Nueces River. These ranches also served to defend the northern *frontera,* despite their remoteness and limited manpower.

The ranch proved ideal as a remote defensive unit. It produced beef, mutton, horses, and wool. Each ranch branded its livestock and allowed them to graze freely on the open range. Tejanos, then, depended on the brand as opposed to fences to delineate ownership between the herds. And on the open range, the horses and the cattle thus became wild, though not ownerless. Indeed, a Tejano longhorn was an aggressive animal that fought viciously. In time of attack, the ranch was protected by its own workers, or *vaqueros,* who could serve as armed soldiers on a moment's notice. Another advantage was that the ranch could be temporarily evacuated to avoid costly sieges or battles. After the attackers left, the ranch owners simply returned to their ranches and resumed operations with minimal losses of livestock or land. Ranching was a system of defensive settlement that the Spaniards had used for a thousand years in Spain and in the New World as well. The major difference was that in Escandon's settlements along the Rio Grande, the *rancho* became a family home, more than simply a livestock and farming operation or a conquest for the Crown. The Nuevo Santander *ranchero,* or principal landowner, seemed to be determined to own the largest ranch in the world—*el rancho grande.*

The settlers who came with Escandon spread quickly onto their ranch lands.

Serrando F. Hinojosa

As soon as Escandon surveyed the new *frontera*, he sent four expeditions out along the Rio Grande. Blas María de la Garza Falcón led one group of settlers, Miguel de la Garza Falcón and Joaquin de Orobio Bazterra led two others, and Escandon himself led a fourth. Between 1747 and 1755, over six thousand colonists drove out from cities in northern Mexico, and quickly founded twenty-three municipalities and fifteen missions.

The major municipalities along the Rio Grande were Laredo, Guerrero, Mier, Camargo, and Reynosa. These five came to be known as Las Villas del Norte, or "the Villages of the North." Guerrero, Mier, Camargo, and Reynosa were founded on the south bank of the Rio Grande, and only Laredo was built on the river's north bank. However, all five municipalities had most of their ranch lands on the north side of the Rio Grande. In the four decades after 1835, a Tejano population of approximately twenty thousand lived in this region on almost one thousand ranches. The ranch families later established such South Texas towns as Dolores, Zapata, Cuevitas, San Diego, San Juan, Palito Blanco, Agua Dulce, El Sauz, Los Olmos, San Luis, Peñascal, San Ygnacio, and Los Saenz.

Decades later, Tejano ranching families still maintained their close ties with their founding families in *Las Villas del Norte*. One of the many twentieth-century descendants of the original settlers of Mier, Alicia Hinojosa, of Zapata, Texas, privately published her own elaborate genealogy, which noted: "All the direct descendants of these first settlers of Mier, are known to be in the thousands." Her genealogy included photos of relatives living throughout South Texas, in cities such as San Antonio, Robstown, and Corpus Christi.[1] Many other Tejano descendants in modern Texas have also published genealogies leading back to the Villas del Norte and, like Hinojosa, can trace their heritage under several flags in Texas, starting with the flag of Spain.

Mexico's independence from Spain in 1821 brought about many changes in boundaries and loyalties. Under the Mexican Constitution of 1824, Nuevo Santander changed its name to Tamaulipas, with its northern boundary still along the Nueces River. North of the Nueces was the new state of Coahuila y Texas. But the settlement patterns of Coahuila y Texas differed greatly from those of Tamaulipas.

Coahuila y Texas attracted Anglo-American settlers into Texas between 1821 and 1835. Immigrant Anglo capitalists set their sights on the region's obvious resources—the vast herds of cattle, the markets in northern Mexico, and the navigable waters of the Rio Grande. The river's upper headwaters were a conduit for the Santa Fe trade in New Mexico, and the Lower Rio Grande, with its mouth at the Gulf Coast, connected the entire region to international markets.

In 1835, Texas challenged Mexico for its independence and became the independent Republic of Texas the following year. The Texas Republic was dominated by Anglo-American capitalists, who immediately laid claim to the Rio Grande from its headwaters to its mouth at the Gulf. The Tejanos, the native Mexicans who had originally established Texas, found themselves in an unusual situation with the Anglo settlers after 1836. During the Texas Revolution, most Tejanos had joined the opposition to the centralist Mexican government of General Santa Anna. But many Anglos in the Republic of Texas quickly forgot that Tejanos had also fought for Texas' independence. Most Anglo-Texans distrusted Tejanos, particularly after Santa Anna massacred the Anglo rebels in the Alamo and at Goliad. After the Anglo-Texan army defeated Santa Anna at the Battle of San Jacinto in 1836, peace was tenuous. In fact, the new republic never fully controlled the region that it claimed south of the Nueces River.

Instead, during the years of the Texas Republic, the Mexicans north of the Rio Grande were attacked by Anglos as well as by Mexican armies. The Mexican armies abused them as traitors, and Anglos never accepted them as fellow Texans. One of the ironies of Texas history is that the original Tejano families, who by this time had been in Texas for almost one hundred years, were still considered "Mexicans" by the Anglos, implying that they were foreigners in the Texas Republic. On the other hand, Anglos who had been in Texas for no more than a few weeks called themselves "Texans." Thus, Tejanos had to defend themselves from newly arrived Anglo Americans who treated them as foreigners. All the while, the political instability invited constant raiding by hostile Apache and Comanche Indians from western Texas. Under these conditions, most Tejanos in the Nacogdoches, Goliad, and San Antonio de Béxar regions permanently lost their ranches. In the region south of the Nueces River, many Tejano ranchers retreated across the Rio Grande, temporarily evacuating their livestock and their families. Tejanos could not use their land, and Anglo-American capitalists could not exploit the river trade.

In effect, the trans-Nueces region of South Texas became a derelict province for many years after 1836. The Anglo-dominated Republic of Texas claimed the territory, but its lands were owned by *rancheros* who still held their land claims under the jurisdiction of their home municipalities, Las Villas del Norte. In an attempt to fill the void of government, one Rio Grande *ranchero*, Antonio Canales, plotted with federalist leaders of the Villas del Norte, including Antonio Zapata, José María Carbajal, and Bernardo Gutiérrez de Lara, to organize an armed insurrection and declare the Independent Republic of the Rio Grande. In 1839 and 1840, under Canales's leadership, a small army of independent *rancheros* claimed control of the Seno Mexicano region, from the Nueces south along the Gulf Coast to Ciudad Victoria in Tamaulipas. The Mexican army suppressed Canales's uprising, but the incident clearly illustrated the lack of a legitimate government in the region during those years.[2] The Republic of Texas simply could not control the land, and Mexico refused to concede the loss.

The controversy with Mexico escalated in 1845, when Texas agreed to be annexed by the United States. Texas claimed the Rio Grande, but Mexico rejected that claim and stationed its army on the river's south bank, at Matamoros. The United States sent General Zachary Taylor and an army of 3,554 men to the Lower Rio Grande region, where they bivouacked at the Mexican village of Corpus Christi, at the mouth of the Nueces River. As the opposing armies maneuvered for position, Mexican troops fired on U.S. troops who were on the north side of the Rio Grande. On hearing of the skirmish, American President James K. Polk declared the attack an act of aggression on American land and ordered Taylor to march toward the Rio Grande. In 1846 Taylor's army took a stand across from Matamoros and engaged Mexican General Mariano Arista in a battle near present-day Brownsville, beginning the Mexican War.

The *rancheros* south of the Nueces still considered themselves to be Mexicans, defending their home Villas del Norte along the Rio Grande, though their primary allegiance was to the municipalities rather than to the government of Mexico. Even Texas Revolution hero Juan N. Seguin of San Antonio de Béxar supported Mexico in that war. Nonetheless, many of the *rancheros* felt that Mexico had neglected and exploited them economically and had little gratitude for the settlers' constant defensive warfare against hostile American Indians on the *frontera*. In another attempt to establish an independent Rio Grande Republic, in 1846 Antonio Canales organized about five hundred *rancheros* from the ranches of Guerrero on the Rio Grande and, just before the outbreak of the war, offered his services to General Taylor. When Taylor declined the offer, which would have required him to recognize the region as an independent republic, Canales's troops joined the Mexican army and became auxiliary troops against Taylor. The *ranchero* cavalry squadron, called the Escuadron Auxiliares de Las Villas del Norte, fought only until Taylor's army evacuated the Villas del Norte on its march southward into the interior of Mexico. Then they evidently disbanded and returned to their ranches north of the Rio Grande for the duration of the Mexican War.[3]

The Treaty of Guadalupe Hidalgo marked the end of war on February 8, 1848, and established the Rio Grande as the southern boundary of Texas and the United States. By virtue of the treaty, Mexican citizens north of the Rio Grande became American citizens, forever separated from their Mexican citizenship and four of their Villas del Norte. Only Laredo, the one Villa on the river's north bank, came under the U.S. flag.

Few of the ranch families were eager to lose their formal ties to Mexico. In Laredo, the town council wrote a letter to the American military commander, Mirabeau B. Lamar, requesting that Laredo be returned to the jurisdiction of Mexico. But Lamar tersely told them to accept the fact that "Mexico has lost Laredo forever."[4] At least the *rancheros* of Laredo were in the same country as their old municipality, making them more fortunate than their neighbors in that respect. Mexico was now across the international border for most of the other *rancheros* and their families. They were technically Americans, but their eyes and their hearts would for many decades remain fixed on their traditional ties with the Mexican Villas del Norte.

From that moment forward, these pioneers lost not only their citizenship as Mexicans, but their very identity. Noted author Américo Paredes cites the Treaty of Guadalupe Hidalgo as "the final element" in defining the new identity of the Mexicans north of the Rio Grande.[5] After many decades as the northernmost bastions of the Spanish *frontera* and a quarter-century as citizens of the Republic of Mexico, they suddenly were citizens of Texas, separated by citizenship from their families in the Villas del Norte. They shared a common cultural heritage with the original Tejano settlers of San Antonio de

Béxar and the other old municipalities of Texas, however, and after the Treaty of 1848—whatever their reservations—they were Tejanos. As Tejanos, they would build on their Mexican heritage as they strengthened their ranch community's ties under a new government.

The Mexican War finally brought a semblance of order to the Rio Grande frontier. The U.S. Army built military forts along the river, and Lamar and other commanders established the American system of county government in place of the Mexican municipalities. The military transportation and quartermaster system built the foundation for a civilian market system—something the Texas Republic could never realize. Although sporadic conflicts continued in the region until the end of the Civil War, the Mexican War successfully laid the capitalist infrastructure that finally gave South Texas access to international markets.

The war had helped make Anglo-Texans and other American soldiers familiar with the Lower Rio Grande Valley, and at its end, many Anglos used their exclusive contacts with the U.S. Army supply system to exploit the region's abundant opportunities for trade and ranching. Steamboat captains such as Richard King, Mifflin Kenedy, James O'Donnell, and Charles Stillman were able to purchase Taylor's surplus river craft after the war, and the Anglo newcomers soon established a veritable monopoly over the robust river trade. Anglo merchants who had contracted as suppliers to Taylor's quartermaster system also reaped sizable profits. These merchants included Col. Henry Kinney at Corpus Christi and Henry Clay Davis, who mustered out of the army at Camargo and established his business at Rio Grande City. By 1848, riverboats, ferries, and military roads linked the Rio Grande hinterland to the Gulf of Mexico. American troops in the Lower Rio Grande Valley also built forts and roads to strengthen their military hold. One of these military roads ran north-south through present-day Willacy County; the other major one paralleled the Rio Grande on the north bank. Used for many years after the war to move troops along the river as well as for the Tejano ranch trade, this road came to be known in the Lower Rio Grande as the Old Military Highway.

In order to secure a stable government for the Lower Rio Grande region, American merchants and government officials established Webb, Starr, and Cameron counties. On January 24, 1852, County Commissioner E. D. Smith, Dr. E. T. Merriman, and area *rancheros* joined to create Hidalgo County from the western half of Cameron County. Merriman, a surgeon who had mustered out of Taylor's army, had bought the large Santa Anna and Alamo land grants. Joining him and Smith to sign the county charter were Sixto Dominguez, owner of Rancho Ojo de Agua; Yndalecio Dominguez, owner of Rosario de Guadalupe Ranch; and Mariano Munguia, who signed with an

"X." A site opposite Reynosa was later selected as the county seat and named Edinburg by two Scotsmen—John Young and John McAllen—who owned the surrounding land.[6]

County designation, however, failed to bring lasting peace, for violence and rebellion occurred continuously. Indeed, the county system ushered in a host of new problems for the Lower Rio Grande region. The major result was a new Anglo-dominated economy and local, state, and national government policies that facilitated transfers of land from Tejano land grantees into Anglo hands. Anglo merchants, land investors, and land lawyers systematically acquired vast Tejano land holdings through capitalist takeovers, through their privileged position in the new county government structure, and occasionally through violence.

The county clerk and tax assessor systems were foreign to the Mexican *rancheros*. The Spanish municipalities traditionally allowed landowners to keep their own land titles at home and to pay user taxes. Tejanos were unfamiliar with the Anglo-Saxon land laws, which required that they submit their treasured land titles to the county clerk and provide proof of annual tax payments. Many of them refused to give up their land titles to Anglos, regardless of the county law. By refusing to comply with the new system, the *rancheros* exposed themselves to illegal proceedings by unscrupulous individuals who wished to dispossess the Tejanos of their lands. Some Anglo land lawyers and county officials quickly amassed vast land holdings from the unregistered *porciónes*.

In his book, *Anglos and Mexicans in the Making of Texas*, David Montejano describes the process that Anglo merchants and land lawyers used to acquire Tejano lands. The most successful land lawyers included James Wells, James Powers, and Robert Kleberg. Montejano cites Cameron County, where by 1882, eighteen Anglos had acquired over a million acres of land—more than four times as much as the Tejano land holdings.[7] The land records of Hidalgo County indicate a similar trend, as some Anglo county officials, including Judge Thaddeus Rhodes of Edinburg, used their positions to press sheriff's auctions against Tejanos who were in arrears on their taxes.[8]

Montejano's book states that the Tejano landowners in South Texas attempted to establish a "Peace Structure" with incoming Anglos to prevent further violence and capitalist takeovers. The Tejanos tended to throw their support to friendly Anglos in official positions of the new counties in a tacit exchange for favorable treatment. Probably just as important, they allowed selected Anglos to marry into some of the wealthiest Tejano families. Intermarriage proved to be a valuable means for Anglo war veterans to penetrate the close-knit families of the old *porciónes*. Judge Rhodes, who was called "Teodoro" by the local Tejano families and had befriended some of the wealthy

Mexican *rancheros* in the Hidalgo County area, in 1852 married Rafaela Hernández, the daughter of the wealthy Mexican owner of La Palma Ranch, south of Matamoros, and took veritable command over much of the Hernández extended family as well as the Tejano ranch workers on his land. Political marriages had been a well-established practice among Mexican families in the Villas del Norte before Anglos arrived; many Tejano families simply continued it with wealthy or powerful Anglos. The wealthy Hinojosa and the Ballí families of Reynosa also married their beautiful daughters to Anglos in hopes of thereby retaining economic and political power under the new order.

A classic example of intermarriage was the case of Petra Vela Vidal of Mier, who married a U.S. Army veteran, Mifflin Kenedy of Downington, Pennsylvania, after he mustered out of Taylor's army. She brought her five children from a previous marriage to the present-day Kenedy County area, where she and Kenedy had five children of their own and established one of the largest ranches in Texas history as Kenedy bought the San Salvador de Tule Spanish land grant, then the Laureles Ranch, and later La Parra Ranch.[9]

As Anglo-American capitalists and land speculators stimulated a growing demand for Tejano lands, the state legislature sent two commissioners throughout the Tejano ranching frontier to clear the titles to as many Tejano lands as possible. William H. Bourland and James B. Miller were authorized by a state law of February 8, 1850, to examine the validity of Tejano land titles and submit their recommendations to the state General Land Office. Neither commissioner nor any of the General Land Office staff had a working knowledge of Spanish, and many Tejano landowners distrusted the Anglo land lawyers and government officials. Indeed, in his letter to the governor, Miller wrote that Tejanos believed that "the board was devised to destroy, rather than to protect their rights." The state's interest was clearly to facilitate land transfers from the old Tejano land-holding families into Anglo hands. From South Texas, Miller wrote to Governor P. H. Bell recommending "some action should be had immediately as the Mexicans are anxious to sell a portion of their land and the Americans equally anxious to purchase . . . ; they can purchase on better terms than they can sue it out through the Courts." The governor promised quick release of the titles to expedite the sale of the Tejano lands.

After collecting as many titles as they could on their river tour from Laredo through Rio Grande City to Brownsville, the commissioners loaded the century-old Spanish titles into a trunk and boarded the Steamship *Anson* at Brownsville for the voyage to Austin. What happened next was a traumatic event that struck deep into the hearts of Tejanos' attitudes toward their new government. In November 1850, the steamship *Anson* sank off the coast of Matagorda, and Miller's next letter to Governor Bell stated that he had "lost my trunk containing all of the original titles presented at Brownsville." The commissioners were forced, as they said, "to procure duplicates and other evidence of the lost titles and documents," relying on bits and pieces of maps, documents, and sworn affidavits.[10] The state legislature eventually validated many of the original Tejano land titles, though many titles were never perfected. With this incident, the credibility of government officials was dealt a setback with the Tejano community.

One result of the rapid transfer of lands was discontent among many Tejanos who had lost their land grants. One of these, Juan Cortina of Cameron County, became a notorious Tejano rebel who raided ranches throughout the Rio Grande Valley during 1859 and after. He was pursued by Texas Ranger John S. "Rip" Ford and by Lt. Col. Robert E. Lee of the U.S. Army, who in the years before the Civil War patrolled the region from Rio Grande City to Brownsville in pursuit of such rebels. To many Tejanos, Cortina was a hero; to the Anglos, he was a bandit. In either case, the "Cortina War" made ranching hazardous in South Texas for many years after 1859.

During the Civil War, river commerce increased along the Lower Rio Grande. A Union blockade of southern shipping ports stimulated steamboat traffic during the war, as troops and raiders used the Old Military Highway, the river fords, and ferries along the Rio Grande extensively. But South Texas avoided the major battles that devastated other southern states, and after the war, steamboat captains like Richard King and Mifflin Kenedy converted their capital into vast land holdings. With access to capital and to contracts with the growing market for Tejano beef in the United States, the Anglo ranch operations became enormously profitable.

During these turbulent times, two separate and unrelated government commissions collected testimony and statistics on the events in South Texas between roughly 1850 and 1875. In 1860, the Secretary of War submitted a report to the United States House of Representatives entitled "Troubles on the Texas Frontier." In 1873, the Republic of Mexico's *Comisión Pesquisidora* or Investigative Commission published a compilation of statistics and sworn statements from Tejanos in the Lower Rio Grande region. Considered together, these two reports offer a rare insight into the violence and lawlessness that prevailed along the border. While anonymous groups of bandits robbed travelers and rustled cattle, many organized forces helped to put pressure on the Tejano ranch families as well. As will be detailed more thoroughly in the epilogue, the Texas Rangers operated from their headquarters on the King Ranch, representing King and other Anglo ranchers. The *Comisión Pesquisidora* reported that King and Hidalgo County Judge Thaddeus Rhodes both financed named individuals who rustled cattle and terrorized small Tejano ranchers. Without protection from Anglo authorities, Tejano ranchers such as Santos Benavides and Santiago Vidaurri eventually had to lead small mounted bands out of the Laredo area to protect their business interests and the landed families who profited from free trade across the border. As both reports show, there was great pressure on the Tejano ranchers to flee the violence or to sell their lands.

By the 1880s, several factors combined to alter radically the Tejano ranchers' hold on their lands in South Texas. Tejanos did not have access to capital as King, Kenedy, and other Anglo capitalists did. According to one study of the records of H. P. Drought & Co. in San Antonio, "During the period from about 1885–1908, out of hundreds of loans only thirty-nine were made to the Mexican *rancheros* south of the Nueces River."[11] Tejanos steadily lost their lands to Anglo ranchers and investors, particularly in time of drought and cold weather. Not all Tejano ranchers lost their lands, of course; some have held on throughout the twentieth century. But their predominance as ranchers in South Texas, their way of life, and their rural community became almost insignificant under the county government structure and Anglo control of capital.

The loss of Tejano lands was particularly ironic because these were the families who had established the so-called "Cattle Kingdom" in the first place. The Cattle Kingdom included the over five million longhorn cattle that the Tejano ranchers and their ancestors had brought into South Texas. The livestock which numbered 85,000 cattle, horses, and mules in 1757, when the early Spaniards established ranching along the Rio Grande, increased to approximately 800,000 by 1795, including 111,777 cattle. These cattle became the major herds of the United States after the end of the Civil War, when cattle drives took millions of these animals north to the railheads in Kansas and Colorado.

Since the founding of the ranching frontier under José de Escandon in the mid-1700s, life had always been a defensive struggle for the *rancheros* and their families. Whether they were fighting the enemies of the Spanish *frontera* or the nebulous forces of capitalism under the American market system, the *rancheros* used their traditional culture for unity and strength. Anglo ranchers had the support of San Antonio bankers and the Texas Rangers, but they did not have such a strong claim on the tradition of ranch life as did the Tejano ranch families. In a state that boasts a frontier tradition, Tejanos were the first among pioneers, and they played a major role in giving Texas its longhorns, its mustangs, and its large ranches. The ranch was their life from the founding of the *frontera* until the close of the nineteenth century. As the following chapters will show, notwithstanding all its difficulties during the early and midnineteenth century, ranch life was an organizing principle for the Tejano communities in South Texas.

Tejano Empire

CHAPTER I

Las Villas del Norte

The nineteenth-century Tejano ranching frontier was born as Tejano ranchers moved into present-day South Texas from two directions. The pioneer families of the Villas del Norte along the Rio Grande began to move northward across the river between the 1790s and 1810. The other direction of movement was from the north, as the original Tejanos from around the San Antonio-Goliad region moved southward fleeing the violence after the Texas Revolution.

The original Tejano ranches along the San Antonio River region were "the cradle of Texas ranching," according to historian Jack Jackson in his monumental book, *Los Mesteños*. Ranching had been founded there by the early Tejanos—the families of the Seguin, the Menchaca, and the Navarro—who built Texas as a *frontera* province. But these ranches declined rapidly during the turbulent years after 1836. Tejano heroes like Juan N. Seguin were forced to hide on their old ranches as a wave of Anglo-American settlers moved into the San Antonio region. Within a few years, even Seguin had to leave his ranch and flee to Mexico.[1] Few Tejano ranchers remained in the San Antonio region after 1836. Likewise, except for the descendants of a few prominent families like the de Leons and the de la Garzas, most Tejanos from Victoria and Goliad also abandoned their ranches after 1836. Even their ranch houses were destroyed, leaving very few original structures. Only a few ranch families remained in the Refugio area, on the north bank of the Nueces River.

Thus, following the Texas Revolution, Tejano ranching shifted southward to the more sparsely populated land between the Nueces River and the Rio

Grande. In this trans-Nueces region, the Tejano ranches underwent their strongest growth surge after 1836. Unlike the San Antonio region, which Anglo Americans quickly dominated, the trans-Nueces region had little appeal to the Anglo Americans for a variety of reasons.

The new Tejano ranching frontier had a semiarid climate and a mostly treeless terrain that was not suited to early nineteenth-century farming. The heat and vast distances between the rural communities seemed to discourage most visitors, except Tejanos. Early travelers commented negatively about the rocky terrain, covered by miles of tall grasses and dense scrub brush which Tejanos called *chaparral*. The grass was about two feet high, although some patches were reportedly "breast high to a man on horseback." Tejanos called this grass *sacate de bestia,* or "beast grass," probably because the wild longhorn cattle thrived in it. Most of the shrubs that made up the chaparral were thorny or had thin foliage. They were not tall enough to afford shade for a traveler, but they were tall enough to obscure a rider's view of the way, and usually very thickly intertwined. One Catholic missionary described the chaparral as a labyrinth that drew bewildered travelers to their death. In his journal, the Abbé Domenech warned: "The Chaparral in which we passed the night, had been fatal to many a colonist who went there to gather wood or nuts. One of the first missionaries of the colony lost his way in it, and was never afterwards heard of. Those who went to look for him, found the bleached skeletons of many colonists who had come by their death there."[2]

Distance was another disorienting feature of the South Texas chaparral. In his journal, Domenech noted that Tejanos seemed to accept great distances as a minor inconvenience. He indicated that when Tejanos told him something was near, he quickly learned to assume that it must be a great distance away. In his own words, the wary visitor said that for Tejanos, "The word near . . . often means 'very far.'"[3] Tejanos, however, seemed to be as blind to the chaparral as fish to water. Like their ancestors who had founded the original Villas del Norte, Tejanos braved the new terrain and established a thriving ranch community that stretched over hundreds of miles of the chaparral.

Since the 1740s, the pioneers of the Villas del Norte had regularly crossed into the depopulated lands north of the Rio Grande to quarry salt from the large salt lake called El Sal del Rey, located in present-day Hidalgo County, a few miles north of Edinburg. They crossed the Rio Grande at a shallow point in the river, using a ferry, or *chalan*. The crossing point was known as Los Ebanos, for its unique ebony trees that overhung the river's north bank and served as an anchor for the *chalan*.[4] For over two hundred years, Los Ebanos welcomed passage to the north.

Some of the first pioneers of Tamaulipas to establish permanent residence on the north bank came from the *villa* of Guerrero, which at that time was still called by its Spanish municipality name, Revilla. As early as 1780, Captain José Miguel de Cuellar crossed the Rio Grande and established his ranch on the north bank. The captain named his ranch El Capitaneño for his military rank. On his ranch, he built some of the earliest stone buildings in present-day Texas. Captain Cuellar was followed the next year by José Eugenio Ramirez, a prominent land grantee from the jurisdiction of Guerrero, who moved in to claim his *Porción* Number 18 on the north bank. Ramirez named the Falcón Ranch after the prominent family name of his wife, Maria Rita de la Garza Falcón. María Rita's family was from the Congregación de Refugio, now called Matamoros, further downstream. As they built the Falcón Ranch for their four sons and two daughters, Don José and Doña Rita became the patriarch and the matriarch for over one hundred family members and workers. By 1800, the Falcón Ranch had its own chapel, its own school, and six business establishments.[5] It began to take on the features of a model Tejano ranch.

The Tejano ranch of the 1800s typically was a family business, operated on land claimed under the state, although the state changed several times during the century. Some Tejanos had land grants from the Crown of Spain for service on the *frontera*. Those who claimed their lands after 1821 received their grants from the Republic of Mexico. Others claimed their lands from the Republic of Texas, and still others as Bounty and Donations for service to the Confederate States of America in the Civil War. But whether their lands were obtained under one flag or another, Tejanos almost all claimed their lands under the legal programs of the government. Few of them borrowed money to buy land as a speculative investment, and no Tejano family is known to have claimed a title in the county land records after killing the original landowner. When the Tejano family worked on the land or prayed on a Sunday morning under a sprawling *encino* oak, they did so on their own ranch, which gave them a strong commitment to the land. Their ownership and pride is reflected in the descriptive names they gave to their ranches, and in the determined stand they took to protect their lands.

A Tejano ranch was run by a patriarch, usually the oldest family male, who conducted the business and protected the family against attack, whether from hostile American Indians or from bandits. For religious instruction, for education, and for order in the household, however, the ranch family looked to the matriarch. Ranch families were usually very large, and though they lived in houses scattered across the ranch, they were often related under an extended family surname. In fact, they usually owned the land in common under a single title, rather than partitioning its ownership among the many members. Family members depended on each other for their economic and social welfare.

They played together, they prayed together, and they worked jointly on major ranch construction and operations.

Most Tejano family ranches were livestock businesses that raised cattle, sheep, goats, and burros for their own use and for market. They also raised minor animals such as hogs and chickens, and they all had extensive gardens of beans, squash, and corn. A single ranch homestead included a main house called a *casa mayor,* often made of stone or caliche blocks called *sillar,* and often smaller homes such as the one-room hut called a *jacal,* with a thatched roof and walls made of logs vertically driven into the ground. Many Tejano ranch homesteads also had a well, an outdoor chimney for cooking, a covered patio, wooden fences, and an oven or brick kiln. Large stock wells with long watering troughs and man-made dams and reservoirs were often near the home as well. The larger ranches also built their own chapels and schoolhouses. Most of the construction was done by the family members and hired workers, though they often brought in an expert to supervise design and construction.

Tejanos used strong construction materials, such as mesquite logs, *sillar* blocks, and stones, which helped the ranch houses to withstand attack. An excellent example of this defensive construction was on the ranch of the Vela family, who had come onto the north bank of the river to claim their land grant *Porción* Number 29 of the Guerrero jurisdiction. They built an extensive homestead of large, flat flagstones called *lajas,* which they took from a quarry on the Rio Grande. In fact, the family built six stone houses on their ranch, which they named La Lajita. The main family house was a two-story structure with stone towers that were reportedly "rounded and topped by parapets." The house had a flat, reinforced roof and served as a fortress against marauders. Indeed, the builders placed firing ports, called *troneras,* in the stone walls, so that family members could aim a weapon outward. The firing ports gave testimony to the frequency and severity of attacks on the early Tejano ranches. One neighboring rancher, Don Benito Ramirez, actually built a fort on his Lopeño Ranch along with his stone house and chapel.

Another wealthy *ranchero* from Guerrero, Don Jesús Treviño, established an extensive ranch that eventually was incorporated as the South Texas town of San Ygnacio. Treviño, who bought his land in 1830 from the original José Vasquez Borrego land grant of the old Revilla jurisdiction, built a stone fort surrounded by a walled courtyard to fend off hostile Indian attacks. At the same time, on a tract where early settlers had attempted unsuccessfully to found the town of Dolores, Cosme Martinez built a substantial ranch with several stone buildings, a well, and a cemetery. He called his ranch Nuevo Dolores, or New Dolores.

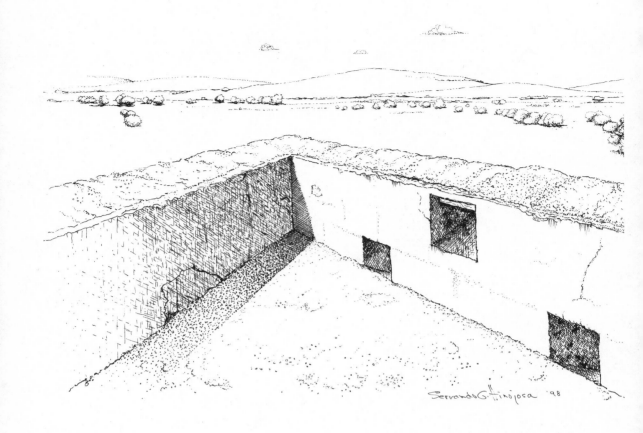

By 1850, there was a sizable permanent ranching community as an extension of old Guerrero. José Luis Ramirez and his wife Basilia Martinez had crossed the river in 1810 to found their ranch, El Ramireño. And in 1822 the Uribe family had founded El Uribeño, also called Las Corrientes de Golondrinas, or "The Flow of Swallows" for the swallows that often made their seasonal mud nests on the mesquite ceiling beams of the stone houses. The peaceful name, however, tended to belie the constant threat of attack. Hostile American Indians often forced the early ranchers to temporarily evacuate their homesteads and retreat across the river to Guerrero. The ranchers did not actually abandon their land, of course, and ordinarily they returned to resume their ranching life and operations after a few months. In this way, courageous Tejano families challenged the barren landscape that other pioneers may have seen as inhospitable to human life.[6]

An example of the Tejano ability to conquer the challenging environment was most evident in the settlement of Los Ojuelos ranch, located in one of the most arid regions of South Texas. The region is a bleak, hundred-mile stretch along a present-day highway in northeast Webb and Jim Hogg counties, north-

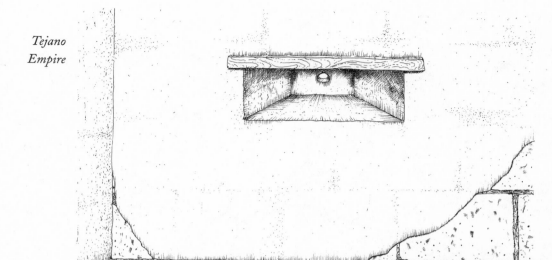

east of Laredo, where the temperatures frequently exceed 100 degrees Fahrenheit for much of the year. The land is characterized by a sparse vegetation of thin shrubs and few trees, with intermittent gullies or arroyos that are usually dusty and dry. It must have appeared as uninviting to nineteenth-century pioneers as to twentieth-century highway travelers. Indeed, on modern Texas highway maps, the area is superimposed by a printed notice warning drivers about the lack of gasoline or service facilities.

Los Ojuelos is at the base of a ridge on the eastern edge of a shallow valley. The early pioneers called this wide, shallow depression a *bajío* and the bordering ridge *el bordo*. On a hot summer day a dusty haze hangs over the entire *bajío,* but on a clear day, the view from *el bordo* reveals the tops of distant mountains far to the south, in Mexico. The *bajío* has never invited a dense population, but Los Ojuelos, at one time, was a veritable oasis. It hosted visitors in its cool, clear pools of natural spring water and even served in the mid-nineteenth century as a birthing center where midwives delivered babies for families from the surrounding ranches. The Tejano pioneers eventually left when Texas Rangers made the ranch a ranger station, and the pools went dry after the petroleum industry pumped and polluted the underground aquifer in the early twentieth century. But the old houses of *sillar* have survived the ravages of time for the better part of two centuries.

Los Ojuelos was first mapped by Eugenio Gutiérrez, who came north from Guerrero in 1810 to claim his land grant of two leagues (approximately 8,856 acres). As Spaniards had always done before him on the semiarid Iberian Peninsula and in northern Mexico, Gutiérrez followed the valley's ridge, *el bordo*, in hopes of finding an escarpment—a ridge line where the earth's tectonic plates had broken, often allowing the underground waters of the aquifer to spring up through one of the breaks. As the water pooled in the rock formation, it created a natural spring which in Spanish is called *el ojo de agua*, or "the eye of water." The early Spanish explorers had followed the Balcones Escarpment from San Antonio de Béxar in a northeasterly direction toward Nacogdoches. Along the escarpment, they found the source of the San Antonio River at San Pedro Springs, the San Marcos Springs in San Marcos, and Barton Springs in present-day Austin. The escarpment that Gutiérrez discovered came to be called Las Bordas Escarpment. At one point on the sharp, rocky ridge is a towering vertical formation of rocks about twenty feet high called "Las Torrecillas" or "The Little Towers." And to his fortune, there was a break in the earth's plates where an underground formation of volcanic ash called Catahoula tuff allowed water to filter up, forming natural springs at the base of the escarpment. Indeed, Las Torrecillas stood in a shallow pool of crystal clear water. Gutiérrez named one of these natural springs Los Ojuelos, the Little Eyes.

He was not able to build permanent structures on his land, however, because hostile American Indians forced him to evacuate it. Gutiérrez returned to Guerrero with a map of his land grant and never returned personally to his land. Back in Guerrero, his daughter, Petra, married Ignacio Guerra and had three sons—Dionicio, José María, and Juan—who set out from Guerrero years later with their grandfather's old map to search for the natural springs and settle his land grant. After they made camp one night, José María, while searching for firewood, found an old cow trail that would logically lead to a watering hole. The following day, according to Guerra family legend, the brothers searched until sundown, when at last they found their grandfather's "promised land."

With a reliable source of water, the Guerra family successfully settled Los Ojuelos as a ranch. They mined *sillar* blocks from the nearby hillsides and used it to build several homes, arranged in two rows to enclose the springs and protect them from Indian raids. By the 1850s, the Rancho Los Ojuelos had expanded to over 20,000 acres. The family encouraged immigration from Guerrero and the Villas del Norte, and the ranch's population increased to over four hundred inhabitants, including the Guerra family, guests, and workers. As the population at Rancho Los Ojuelos grew, other ranchers moved to the surrounding area, and the new ranchers also found natural springs on their lands.[7]

The names of the ranches around Los Ojuelos reflected the abundant underground springs. In 1825, for example, one neighboring ranch was named Las Albercas de Arriba, or the Upper Pools, and another ranch was called Las Albercas de San Felipe, or the San Felipe Pools. The ranch of Guadalupe Canales, built on the escarpment above the Catahoula tuff formation, took the name of the ridge, El Bordo, and boasted the Charco Escondido, or the Hidden Puddle. All of these were reportedly clear-water pools with large perch and flocks of ducks. Indeed, two of the neighboring ranches were called El Pato and El Patito, or The Duck and The Little Duck, respectively. The Vela Cuellar ranch nearby was named La Tinaja, or the Pond, for the water formed by springs that reportedly flowed from a Goliad sand formation and produced water throughout the twentieth century.

All of these early ranches were notable not only for forming a barrier against hostile American Indian raids, but also for creating a pioneering trail into the rugged ranch country across from the Villas del Norte. Though the land was rugged, these Tejano ranchers apparently enjoyed an abundance of plant and animal life. Their homes, particularly around Los Ojuelos, had not only vegetable gardens, but also luxuriant flower gardens and flowering plants such as Texas mountain laurel, anacahuita, and jasmine. Indeed, at some of the early *sillar* homes at Los Ojuelos, where descendants of the original Guerra family still lived as late as the 1990s, the water wells were still flowing, and the jasmine vines still produced fragrant white blossoms over 186 years after Eugenio Gutierrez first found the springs. Another surviving feature of the ranches at Los Ojuelos was the cemetery, located on the crest of the *bordo* that overlooks the *bajío*. The graves were interspersed among flowering guajillo shrubs and several huge boulders at the surface of the outcropping, near the ridge of the escarpment. The cemetery symbolized the Tejanos' love for the peculiar foliage and the unique terrain of their *frontera*.

A few miles west of Los Ojuelos, the elusive monarch butterfly migration brought clouds of the colorful butterflies on their annual flight to the mountains of Mexico to the south. According to biologist Arturo Longoria's *Adios to the Brushlands,* monarch butterflies were following migratory underground pathways called *ramaderos,* which were corridors of "fifty-yard wide emerald ribbon, where trees and shrubs reached three times the height of the surrounding vegetation, marking the route of a slow moving, sub-surface stream." Longoria states that the summer ground temperature above the *ramaderos* could be as much as ten degrees lower, thus luring the butterflies on their winding pathways through the Tejano ranch frontier.[8] With its cool spring waters, jasmine blossoms, and butterflies, Los Ojuelos and the surrounding ranches offered their own natural beauty for the determined Tejano pioneers. The barren *bajío* periodically rewarded them as well, when the normally quiet-colored sage, guajillo, and cactus suddenly burst into colorful bloom after a desert rain.

East of the ranches around Los Ojuelos, another migration of rancheros moved northward from their municipality of Ciudad Mier. Led by Don Hipolito García, the Mier pioneers moved as far north as present-day San Diego and Sandia on the south bank of the Nueces River. Don Hipolito was born in Mier in 1816 and settled his ranch, El Randado, in his early twenties. He married Doña Andrea Montalvo García, and they had a daughter, Margarita. When Don Hipolito founded it, El Randado consisted of 45,000 acres, but the ranch encompassed over 100,000 acres by the time he died in 1888. As a livestock ranch, El Randado prospered and excelled in the production of horses, sheep, cattle, and goats, and became a landmark. At Don Hipolito's death, Margarita's husband, Bernardo de la Garza, succeeded him as the ranch patriarch.[9]

By that time, El Randado was a sizable village with over 150 family members, guests, and workers, several *sillar* homes and other buildings, its own San Rafael Chapel (built by Doña Andrea), a commissary store, and eventually its own post office. The ranch cemetery, which was quite large for a family ranch, centered on the large stone tomb of Don Hipolito. One of the most impressive features of the ranch was the man-made dam and reservoir, lined with *sillar* blocks. The ranch also had stock wells that used large buckets to draw water into long watering troughs, also lined with stone or *sillar*. Such a well was called a *noria con buque*, or a "well with bucket," and supported year-round water for the herds of livestock.

With such a large population and a reliable water source, El Randado became a center for artisans. Indeed, one ranch story holds that the ranch actually took its name only after its artisans began to produce ranch crafts. One of the crafts for which the ranch was most renowned was the production of artistically trimmed ropes, such as the decorative lasso called a *randa*, and supposedly the ranch derived the name El Randado for the artistic ropework. A favorite stopping place for travelers, the ranch boasted famous visitors, including Lt. Col. Robert E. Lee of the U.S. Army, who stopped there on a trip to Brownsville just before the outbreak of the Civil War. According to records, Colonel Lee "greatly enjoyed the hospitality of this home." Another of the ranch's claims to fame was that when the town of Hebbronville was incorporated nearby in the twentieth century, El Randado actually had more voters in its old *casas de sillar* than the entire modern town.[10] The old ranch's most significant claim, however, was that in a state that boasts the large ranches of the nineteenth-century "Cattle Kingdom," El Randado was one of the largest, and probably produced more cattle, horses, and sheep for a longer uninterrupted time span than any other ranch in Texas. On El Randado, Don Hipolito was a model of the Texas ranch king that Tejanos as well as Anglo-Americans would emulate.

Another of Don Hipolito's major contributions was in serving as a pathfinder to the northernmost corners of the ranch country. Following his lead, Captain José María Benavides and Ignacio Benavides came north to take possession of the Hinojosa land grant, which their grandfather, Simon de Hinojosa, had received in 1740 under the Spanish crown, or as their Tejano descendants proudly said, "*de la Corona de España.*" On their Noriecitas Ranch, the Benavides brothers built several *casas de sillar,* a large *presa* or dam, and a cemetery. Another ranch near El Randado was Las Cuevitas, or the Little Caves, founded by Sigifredo Muñoz.

Ciudad Mier was one of the old Villas del Norte on the Rio Grande, and its citizens in the 1830s were descendants of Escandon's original land grantees. According to the Abbé Domenech, the families of Mier were physically distinguishable from those of the other *villas*. In his 1851 journal, Domenech wrote: "I observed that in Mier, the people's skin is fairer than in other towns of the frontiers, and both sexes are most strikingly handsome. Their features are regular, delicate, and of a decidedly noble cast; and they speak the Spanish more pure, correct, and less corrupted with Indian words and phrases."[11] Though these pioneers were not clannish, their families tended to stay together as they moved northward along a front about fifty miles wide. One of the most important land grants established by pioneers from Mier was the Rancho San Diego on San Diego Creek. Established by Encarnación García Pérez and Martiana Pérez de García, the ranch quickly came to be known as the Villa de San Diego, and eventually became the present-day city of the same name. It was near the Tinaja de Lara and the Preseños grants, located north of present-day Alice, Texas, near the Nueces River. Juan Baptista González and other settlers soon founded the surrounding ranches like La Rosita and El Palito Blanco. Thirty-five miles south of San Diego, the Peñitas Ranch was also under the *jurisdicción de Mier.*

As the early pioneers of Mier moved northward toward present-day San Diego, their migration was reinforced by a commercial venture from Matamoros, further downstream. In 1832, the Tamaulipas merchants opened commercial relations with the Tejano, Anglo, and Irish colonies located on the north bank of the Nueces River in Texas. The Irish colonists of the McGloin and McMullen settlements were situated in San Patricio, near Refugio. The famous Tejano family of Carlos de la Garza was in the neighboring Victoria municipality with several ranches established on the old Manuel Becerra land grant. The most famous was the Carlos Rancho, which was a Tejano refuge during the Texas Revolution and was reported to be worth $7,000 in 1858. Carlos was surrounded by the successful ranches of his brothers, José María, Paulino, and Francisco. The de la Garza brothers did a brisk trade in cattle and horses, and along with the Anglo and Irish settlers, the de la Garza ranches attracted the business interests of Tamaulipas.

As a friendly gesture, the Matamoros merchants established a trade route northward through present-day Kenedy and Kleberg Counties to San Patricio. They then invited the Texas colonists to meet them on the banks of the Agua Dulce Creek, just south of the Nueces. There, on Saint John's Day, June 24, 1832, they all met for a four-day feast and banquet. The festivities included horse races, dances, and games, but the most noteworthy event, evidently, was the banquet, because the place came to be known as *El Lugar del Banquete*, the Place of the Banquet, near present-day Banquete, Texas. The gesture began a tradition of four-day fiestas there, and it opened a trade route that would later form a major road for Confederate cotton and eventually a U.S. highway.[12] Most importantly, it launched another area of northward expansion from the Villas del Norte.

By 1850, San Diego had become a crossroads for the trade between San Patricio and Brownsville and was on the road from Corpus Christi to Laredo. The San Diego area was a conglomeration of thriving horse, cattle, and sheep ranches—all within a few miles of each other—and each ranch developed with its own *casas,* chapels, and schoolhouses of *sillar.* A traveling Catholic priest described San Diego in 1866 as "a little ranch town of Mexican families . . . [that] lived in small communities six or eight miles apart." Some of the ranches in the San Diego area became quite successful in cattle and sheep production, with the Perez family operations among the largest. Alejos Perez, for example, had over a thousand horses and three thousand sheep on his ranch. Pablo Pérez reportedly had over five hundred cattle and as many sheep on his 11,220-acre spread. Another ranchero in the San Diego area, Albino Canales, had 1,500 horses and 1,500 sheep. The San Diego ranches were notable not only for their commercial success after the 1850s, but also for the large network of closely knit family ranches, including Las Conchas, La Trinidad (sixteen miles from San Diego), Santa Gertrudis, Petronilla, Concepción, La Rosita, Mendieta, Peñitas, Veleño, and Lagarto.[13]

The largest concentration of Tejano ranches expanded northward from Matamoros and from Reynosa, the municipality with the largest jurisdiction of the five Villas del Norte. The families from Reynosa eventually expanded the *frontera* eastward to the Gulf Coast, and then northward to the Nueces River at present-day Corpus Christi. And though they eventually lost much of their acreage to Anglo ranchers and farmers, they were probably the most significant group of Tejano ranchers. They held some of the earliest land grants and created some of the largest of the Tejano ranches, and they were situated in the region that would become the highly populated Lower Rio Grande Valley of the twentieth century. In addition, many of their descendants would be among the wealthiest ranch families of Texas.

Like Tejanos whose families came from Mier and Guerrero, the earliest settlers of the Lower Rio Grande Valley were descendants of the original *porción* grantees. The wealthy families of Reynosa were noted for their ability to claim vast amounts of land and for staging strategic marriages between their families to retain a hold over land, power, and commerce. Captain Juan José Hinojosa, the Chief Justice of Reynosa, started a veritable ranch kingdom when he obtained the enormous Llano Grande *porción* of twenty-five leagues in 1778. Following his example, his son, Vicente Hinojosa, claimed the thirty-five-league Las Mesteñas grant. Then his grandson, Juan José Ballí, claimed the seventy-two-league San Salvador de Tule grant. These early ranch families created the "Rancho Grande" image that Richard King, Mifflin Kenedy, and other ranch "kings" would later imitate. Vicente Hinojosa's Las Mesteñas, for example, eventually spread out to enclose thirty Tejano ranches, and adjoined the 12 1/2-league La Feria grant of his sister, Rosa María Hinojosa de Ballí.[14]

The large families from Reynosa forged links among the Ballí, Hinojosa, Garza, and Cano names to hold their enormous ranches. Little wonder, then, that Anglo names like Kenedy and McAllen would someday weave through the land documents of these same Reynosa estates. Prominent Spanish names traditionally followed the powerful ranches in the *jurisdicción de Reynosa,* and some of these would continue in the modern counties of Cameron, Willacy, and Kenedy, some intermarried with Anglo names.

After the Hinojosa and Ballí families set the pace in the early grants, other Reynosa families followed their example by establishing large ranches as they spread eastward toward the Gulf of Mexico. The move toward the coast was begun by none other than the son of Rosa María Hinojosa de Ballí. Nicolás Ballí, a priest, received a major grant that was later named Padre Island in reference to his religious title. The priest was followed by Eugenio and Bartolomé Fernández, who had a large grant downstream from La Feria. Their estate, the Concepción de Carricitos, was followed in turn by Pedro Villareal, who named his ranch San Pedro de Carricitos. Just to north of the Villareal and Fernández grants was the 106-league San Juan de Carricitos, belonging to

José Narciso Cavazos, which stretched from present-day Willacy County, where Raymondville and Lyford now stand, to the Gulf Coast at Laguna Madre.[15] From this line of estates along the Rio Grande, the Reynosa families then turned northward along the coast, toward the Nueces River.

In the final phase of their expansion, the Reynosa families moved onto their land grants to establish working ranches after the Mexican War. One of the earliest was in the present-day Brooks County area, where Andrés Canales founded his ranch called Las Cabras, or the Goats. His sons later divided the ranch into three major ranches, which they passed on to their twentieth-century descendants. The Canales would be famous for their political leadership among Tejanos at the turn of the century; the family included judges and at least one state legislator. Another famous ranch was that of Petra Vela Vidal of Mier, who married Mifflin Kenedy in 1852. Doña Petra, a wealthy widow, already had children of her own and then had other children with Kenedy. Their marriage combined her acquisitive skills with his access to Anglo-American capital to create one of the largest ranch corporations in Texas.

The Kenedy Ranch was surrounded by several other Tejano ranches that were based on land grants given under the Mexican government of Tamaulipas. The 16,000-acre ranch of Juan Antonio Ballí was located inland and contained groves of oak trees covered with Spanish moss. The moss, with its characteristic paisley twists, was called *paistle,* and the ranch was called El Paistle. Adjoining it was La Atravesada Ranch, on the La Parra land grant that originally belonged to Alvino de la Garza. The matriarch of La Atravesada Ranch was Doña Eulalia Tijerina, who was known and respected by area ranchers for her tenacious resistance to aggressors. Within the over 76,000 acres of the La Parra grant were the other Tejano ranches of Las Labores and La Parra, along present-day U.S. Highway 77 between Harlingen and Kingsville and only a few miles from the Gulf Coast. In her classic study of Tejano ranches, historian Emilia Schunior Ramirez notes that the old Tejanos often referred to the miles of towering sand dunes, called *médanos,* that marked this stretch of ranch land. According to Ramirez, the sand dunes have long since been overgrown with grass, but they are still recognizable as the only hills along that modern highway.

Several other large Tejano ranches covered the area between modern Highway 77 and the Gulf Coast, but these were to fall victim to raids by Anglo bandits, who descended from the King Ranch and Corpus Christi in the 1870s, killing all of the men on the ranches and leaving the ranches with no title holders. As detailed in the epilogue, raids on the Atravesada Ranch of Eulalia Tijerina, the Carrastolendas, the Corral de Piedra, and the Peñascal killed a number of Tejano ranchers and caused others to flee to the Villas del Norte, leaving their lands to be appropriated by Anglo ranchers or sold for a pittance at sheriff's auction.[16]

Other Tejano ranchers survived in the region north of Reynosa, however. Indeed, Ramirez estimated in her study that in 1852 there were between forty and forty-five Tejano ranches within the limits of present-day Hidalgo County alone. Many of these became highly successful business operations. One of the most prosperous ranches, in present-day Cameron County, belonged to the "Spaniard banker," Francisco Yturria. Yturria became an investor in the railroad that later cut through the region, and he built the Yturria railroad depot on his land. Nearby ranches included the Paso Real, which had its own stagecoach stop on the line between Matamoros and San Antonio, and the San Manuel Ranch of Manuel Chapa. Another Tejano landowner who became a successful investor was Macedonio Vela, who with his wife, Mercedes, built their Laguna Seca Ranch fifteen miles north of present-day Edinburg in 1867, and operated a profitable livestock operation. Other successful businessmen were Pedro Longoria, who had a 12,000-acre ranch in Cameron County, and Salvador Guerra in Hidalgo County. Longoria registered 700 horses and 4,400 cattle with the county tax office by the end of the century, and Guerra registered 1,500 sheep.[17] Although the ranchers of the Lower Rio Grande Valley suffered the greatest losses to Anglo bandits and capitalists by the end of the century, many of them also proved to be the most resilient as they adapted to the modern capitalist structure.

Far to the west of Reynosa was Laredo, the only one of the Villas del Norte located on the north bank of the Rio Grande. It had been founded last, and likewise the region's Tejano ranches were some of the last to be established. Fermina Guerra, the historian of Tejano ranches in Laredo, has stated that there were about forty Tejano ranches in the area after 1860. The ranch of Nicolas Sanchez had 7,500 sheep, and that of Ramon Martinez had 10,400 sheep. The Laredo ranches were not the largest of the Tejano working ranches, but they were notable for the stability and the vitality of their family and community networks.

Indeed, the ranches' colorful names gave a strong indication of the lively culture of the region: the San José, the Santa Fe, El Salado, and Las Tinajas meant, respectively, the Saint Joseph, the Holy Faith, the Salty, and the Little Ponds. Some Laredo ranches were named after trees and vegetation: the Alamito for the cottonwood tree, the Palo Blanco for the hackberry, the Nopalosa for the many cactus plants, and the Ortiguilla for the vicious stinging weed peculiar to the area. La Leona was named for a mountain lion, and La Jotena for the "J" brand on unclaimed cattle that roamed the area. La

Cautiva, meaning "The Captive," was named for its owner, a lady who had been captured by Indians. And Las Mujeres Ranch, meaning "The Women," was so named for the ranch family's many daughters. Other ranches were simply named for their owners, including the Mendioleño, the Peraleño, and the Serna families.

All of these ranches belonged to large families who lived in close-knit communities on their ranches. For example, Don Justo Guerra reared his two sons, Carmen and Florencio, on his ranch, and then sent them out in 1870 to build their own ranches adjacent to his. Carmen Guerra founded the Santa Fe Ranch and Florencio Guerra the Buena Vista Ranch, and each became a "don" or a respected owner in his own right. Don Florencio lived with his three sons and seven daughters on 2,800 acres, and had over three hundred cattle in the 1870s. Nearby, Don Casimiro Benavides lived with his eight children on La Becerra Ranch, which had its own commissary store where neighboring Tejano ranch families came to buy food and supplies. La Becerra also served as the mail stop and, more importantly, as the focal point for the surrounding ranch community. Don Casimiro, for example, was the local folk healer or *curandero,* and his ranch hosted the periodic four-day festivals that combined religious observances with horse racing, gaming, and all-night dancing. In many ways, La Becerra symbolized the strong family and community ties among the Laredo Tejano ranches. In terms of acreage it was not the largest ranch in Texas, but it probably had as many family members residing on it as most of the largest Texas ranches. And when the residents looked for a community, they found it on the ranch, not in town. In that way, La Becerra was probably representative of most Tejano ranches of the nineteenth century.

West of Laredo, near present-day Eagle Pass, Don Refugio San Miguel of Matamoros founded "the first ranch in Maverick County" in 1865. Though at the western periphery of the Tejano ranching frontier of South Texas, Don Refugio followed many of the same patterns of construction and ranch operations as his counterparts from the Villas del Norte. The two-story stone house at San Miguel Ranch was surrounded by a high stone wall and featured a stone tower with *troneras* "at advantageous points," making it "a veritable fortress." Don Refugio had hundreds of horses and thousands of sheep and cattle on the ranch, and he also owned a major cart freighting business as a contractor for the U.S. Army's nearby Fort Duncan. Don Refugio and his wife, Doña Rita Alderete, operated the ranch until his death in a bandit ambush in 1868, after which Doña Rita continued both the ranch operations and the cart business. As she reared her six children, her family became an integral part of the Eagle Pass community as well as the surrounding ranch community.[18]

Tejano ranch families were linked not only to other ranches in their local area, but also to the Tejano ranch community throughout the trans-Nueces region. The families from the five municipalities of Laredo, Guerrero, Mier, Camargo, and Reynosa shared common names and a unified cultural heritage. But more importantly, they were dynamically interdependent, economically as well as socially, sharing in common such problems as hostile American Indians, as well as common markets for their livestock. Although the many families of a ranch clustered around the ranch's main family or patriarch, they also formed strong networks with ranch families across the region, maintaining regular communication through a system of pony express lines, stagecoach lines, and mail routes.

The stagecoach lines, called *la diligencia,* that operated through the Tejano ranching frontier were operated either by companies like Wells Fargo or by the ranchers themselves. The stagecoach, usually drawn by two horses, stopped about every fifty miles, at the larger ranches along the route. The exchange stations were called *postas,* or posts, and while the horses were being changed, the passengers stretched, new passengers boarded, and the mail pouch might be exchanged for forward stations. The stagecoach trip was reportedly dusty and slow.

One main line ran from San Antonio through San Diego to Matamoros, and later Brownsville, passing through the Paso Real Ranch, El Sauz Ranch, and Las Yescas Ranch just north of Brownsville in present-day Cameron County. Later, it ran through Alice, ten miles east of San Diego, and the trip from Brownsville to Alice reportedly took a grueling thirty hours. A western line ran northwest from Brownsville along the Rio Grande, through the ranches of Zapata and on to Laredo, and on the Old Military Highway that General Zachary Taylor had used during the Mexican War. One of the main *postas* on the western route was an ancient stopping place called *el tapadero,* or "the meeting place." There, in the 1860s, Oblate priests built a small chapel of *sillar* and called it La Lomita, the Little Hill. In 1877, the landowner, a wealthy merchant of Reynosa, granted the priests two entire *porciónes,* No. 55 and No. 57, for their chapel. The priests, in turn, allowed the stage lines to use mission horses as fresh replacements.

For faster communication, the Tejano ranches used their own pony express. Single, mounted riders carried only one canvas bag for parcels and a smaller leather pouch for letters. The riders sped their ponies on a rigid schedule between *postas,* partially to expedite the mail but also to minimize the risk of interference by hostile American Indians. One of the riders, Andrés Serna of Zapata, said he rode from 6 A.M. until sunset, stopping at the *postas* along his route only to exchange his mount for a fresh one. On particularly long routes, replacement riders were also part of the exchange.[19] The pony express and the stagecoach carried the bulk of the mail for the Tejano ranching frontier until they were finally replaced by the U.S. postal service at the close of the nineteenth century. Until that time, they represented one more example of a dynamic, rugged pioneer society striving to preserve its community through its own resourcefulness.

Texas history books have given scant attention to the Tejano community of this period, and Anglo Americans of the time rarely recorded Tejano society's constructive aspects. The writings of Melinda Rankin, a Methodist missionary, indicate that she arrived in Brownsville in 1859 with strongly biased, preconceived notions of an inferior Mexican society. She noted in her report that she had seen her "first live Mexican" and that her Anglo colleagues had led her to believe that, in their words, "the Mexicans were a people just fit to be exterminated from the earth." Rankin would later form her own, more favorable, impressions of the Mexican culture. Other Anglos reporting on this ranching frontier, however, depicted the Tejanos as lazy, thieving vagrants.

These prejudices, of course, are strongly contradicted by hundreds of property owners who had received formal land titles from the King of Spain and from the Republic of Texas for military service in defense of their government. The prejudices were also contradicted by Tejanas like Doña Rita Alderete, who operated her own ranch and freight contracting business and who undeniably had both financial and spiritual strength. The Tejano ranching frontier was a stable society that operated profitable ranching businesses. And, of course, Tejanos considered Anglos to be the foreigners—in the words of Jovita González, "interlopers, no less than vandals"—in their lands. It is true that Tejanos were not large capitalists with the funding to build corporate ranches—perhaps because they did not have the ready access to capital that Anglo banking institutions gave to Anglos moving into South Texas. Nevertheless, the Tejanos' ranch lifestyle would become the ideal to Anglo-American cattlemen, and the Tejanos' success in producing wool and cattle attracted thousands of dreamers, capitalists, and adventurers from the United States and the world.

Like nineteenth-century Anglo Americans, many modern historians have failed to appreciate the many positive characteristics of Tejano ranches and ranching families. Celebrated historian Terry G. Jordan essentially denied that the Tejano ranching frontier even existed north of the Rio Grande after 1850. Walter Prescott Webb's highly acclaimed book, *The Great Plains,* boasted of the Cattle Kingdom of Texas and memorialized the famous longhorn herds as a Texas phenomenon, but Webb and other historians seldom mention that throughout much of the nineteenth century, many Tejano ranchers had as many sheep as cattle, or that in many counties, sheep outnumbered cattle. In fact, the hundreds of Tejano sheep ranches in the hinterland at one time were called "the greatest wool market in the world," producing millions of pounds of wool annually by 1880 and helping to make Corpus Christi "the nation's largest export point for live sheep."[20]

The five million longhorn cattle that Walter Prescott Webb identified in his book as Texas Longhorns could more appropriately be called Tejano Longhorn. They were brought to Texas by Tejanos, propagated by Tejanos, and many had Tejano brands. When Webb and other historians identified the famous cattle trails in Texas and the cowtowns in Kansas, they specifically identified the Chisholm Trail, the Goodnight-Loving Trail, the Western Trail—names that have been integrated into every U.S. history textbook—and the cowtowns of Dodge City, Sedalia, and Abilene, where the cattle were loaded for shipment to Chicago and the East. American students today learn that American industrial revolution needed the beef for protein. But few history books mention the Tejano ranches like the Tinaja de Lara or the Randado, where millions of those cattle were raised, and no Texas history textbook map yet has ever named the Tejano towns and ranches where the famous cattle trails actually originated. Most historical accounts simply indicate the southern-most Anglo-American town on the trails, on the assumption that the cattle herds actually formed there, when in fact, the Peña Ranch in present-day Jim Hogg County was the real, though so far unacknowledged, southern end—the producing end—of the Chisholm Trail. Likewise, monuments and historical markers at the state capitol and in county courthouse squares across Texas memorialize the Anglo-American cowboy, rather than the Tejano who perfected the cattle drive, the brands, the roundup, and open range grazing. Tejanos were not, as the Anglos sometimes claimed, lazy vagrants who deserved to be exterminated; instead, they were the ranchers whose cattle provided America with the protein to feed its industrial revolution. Long before the Anglo-American cattle kings arrived, Tejanos had already created the legendary western ranch, with its intricate divisions of labor, social order, and systems of work, education, and play.

CHAPTER 2

Life in a Casa de Sillar

The French had their villas on the beaches of the Mediterranean, the Swiss had their chalets, and Americans in the Old South, their plantations. All of these estates tended to reflect the highest ideals of their rural society and were known for their products or for their unique, even idyllic living style. And their owners thought enough of these estates to christen them with names that evoked the saints, such as Villa Marie Therese and the Villa Jean Pierre, or the muses, or perhaps a mythical utopia.

Tejanos had their *ranchos,* estates that produced livestock in a highly distinctive manner. The *ranchero,* the patriarch of that estate, represented the crest of Tejano society. The term "ranchero" simply means rancher, as the owner of the ranch. But because land ownership was a mark of distinction among the *pobladores primitivos,* or primary settlers, the *rancheros* had social status as well. They often were the eldest of the ranch families, and they served the function of political and even military leaders. Indeed, many of the *rancheros* led militia or cavalry squadrons composed of hundreds of vaqueros into battle from time to time. According to Fermina Guerra of Laredo, the *rancheros* had a custom of keeping two homes—one on the ranch and one in town, like the wealthy Don Florencio Guerra, whose twelve-room home in Laredo was the pride of the townspeople. "But the ranch held the center of their affections," she noted.[1] They christened their ranches with names that reflected their family pride, their claim to uniqueness, or their location—Las Albercas de San Felipe, San Salvador del Tule, San Juan de los Lagos, El Ramireño. The Tejano ranch estate on the *frontera* was a family's fortress against hostile elements, their financial security, their fortune. Above all, the ranch was home—*mi casa.*

A Tejano ranch was a veritable complex of buildings, of operations, and of families. A ranch was typically built on a land grant; if the land grant were a large one, it could contain two, three, or several other ranches. Each ranch could be home to several families living as far as a quarter mile or a half mile apart. Though the homes might be separate, the families were usually closely interdependent, functioning as a single household. On some ranches, several homes were clustered within a single courtyard or enclosure. In such cases, the several families jointly or communally owned the land grant in undivided shares. And their daily life revolved around the ranch courtyard.

Tejano ranch life centered on the home. The eldest owner or patriarch lived in the main house, which was called the *casa mayor* and was made of stone or *sillar.* Surrounding the *casa mayor* were smaller log huts called *jacales,* where the patriarch's sons or cousins lived with their families. The *casa mayor* usually had an adjoining patio sometimes covered with an arbor-like roof. Beyond the patio roof—and separate from the home—was a stone chimney for cooking the food. There was also a dome-shaped, stone outdoor oven called an *horno,* which was located away from the house and used not only to bake bread but to fire bricks or burn seashells to produce lime for the ranch. Ranches almost always had a corral or stockade of mesquite logs, either encircling the patio or adjacent to it, for their horses. And always around the house and patio, the ranchers planted their vegetable garden and flowering vines and shrubs.

Most Tejano ranchers built a well, lining it with a rock wall or *sillar* about halfway down the well and two or three feet above ground level. They always planted large shade trees in the outer yard—mesquite if nothing else—and they built an outer stockade or fence about fifty to one hundred feet from the house. The outer stockade served as an enclosure for the ranch yard, to protect small animals and children during the day and to ward off predatory animals at night. Beyond the enclosure were larger stock wells and corrals, as well as other buildings such as a schoolhouse, a commissary store, or a chapel. Also beyond the enclosure lay the family cemetery, though according to Fermina Guerra, it was never more than "a stone's throw behind the ranch house." Usually, the crosses were visible from the patio, beneath a nearby grove of trees. A few ranchers built smaller buildings as sheds for buggies and carriages or for a laundry. At the edge of the enclosure, downwind, they almost always had the *matanza,* or slaughterhouse—usually nothing more than a crude table near a large tree, occasionally with "posts that were used to hang up the slaughtered oxen." In addition to the buildings, some ranch families constructed an earthen dam and reservoir along a nearby arroyo or creek.[2]

All of these were typical features on the Tejano ranches of South Texas during the nineteenth century. They were constructed as time and resources allowed and thus were present in varying degrees on different ranches. On the more developed ranches, all of these features could be present, while on a new ranch, the young settlers might live in a one-room *jacal,* planning to build their *casa de sillar* in the years to follow.

The first step in building the *casa mayor* was to obtain the services of a professional stonemason who would design the house and supervise the construction. In the nineteenth-century Laredo area, for example, when a family was ready to build the *casa mayor,* they called on Trinidad Gonzales. He built ranch houses at La Becerra, the San José, and the Buena Vista ranches, all of which survived well into the twentieth century. The house at Buena Vista reportedly "stood as a white shining landmark" for over a century.[3]

The next step was to bring in the construction materials. Tejano ranchers typically quarried and gathered natural materials from the surrounding area. Sometimes they had rough-cut lumber or wooden beams hauled in from town on carts. In the 1860s, they paid a cart driver forty dollars per trip to haul materials, traveling about ten miles per day over the undeveloped trails. The trip could be expensive if the cart became stuck in the mud while carrying a load of the heavy *lajas,* or large, flat flagstones. In one such incident, the construction of the chapel at San Diego was delayed for many days while the cart drivers waited for the mud to dry.

The ranchers hauled large, flat stone *lajas* from an arroyo or a riverbed, often the Rio Grande. They used the stone to build the home's foundation and floor above ground level. Homes of stone or *sillar* were laid out in a rectangle, approximately sixteen feet long by twelve feet wide, and often larger. After laying the rectangular foundation and floor, the builders constructed the walls of *sillar,* a kind of dense caliche which they cut in massive blocks, two feet long, twelve inches thick, and eighteen inches high, out of a quarry or an exposed hillside. They worked by hand, with a hammer and chisel, then loaded the blocks onto oxcarts and hauled them to the home site. There, they used a lime mortar and smaller stones to stack the blocks evenly on one another to form a wall. The workers then whitewashed the wall inside and out with a smooth paste of sand and lime. The mortar resisted cracking through the years. And the porous *sillar*—crumbly when first quarried—likewise hardened through the years, forming an efficient insulation.[4]

The thick-walled *sillar* houses of the early nineteenth century incorporated *troneras,* or portholes for firing weapons at attackers, as an integral part of the *sillar* wall adjacent to each window or the door. The *troneras* were

specifically pointed so that residents could aim across a predetermined "kill zone" at the entrance to the courtyard.

The roof of an old *sillar* house was one of its most impressive features. The Tejanos used massive, hand-hewn wooden beams called *vigas* to span the entire flat roof. The *vigas* were made of a hard, durable wood like the bald cypress, which they called *sabino* or *ciprés,* or of mesquite. The mesquite is a thin shrub in most of Texas, but in South Texas, it was cultivated as a tall shade tree with thick clumps of leaves that hung much like willow branches. Indeed, General Zachary Taylor selected a stately old mesquite in 1846 to mark the hillside graves for his first wartime casualties in Corpus Christi. Known as the Old Bayview Mesquite, the tree survived well into the twentieth century as one of the largest of that species on record. Both the mesquite and the bald cypress require very little water to survive, and they provided the long *vigas* for many *casas de sillar* such as the nineteenth-century Tejano homes in Zapata and the old chapel at La Lomita, for example.

Because the central beam was so prominent in the ceiling of the home, Tejanos printed timeless inscriptions on the *viga* rather than using a cornerstone to record the home's creation. To the Tejano ranch family, the inscription on the *viga* was their testimony, their immortality, their epitaph. Sometimes, it simply recorded the date, as in the San Diego home where the *viga* said simply: "*Esta casa se acabo en 1876,*" or "This home was finished in 1876." But usually the inscription was more inspirational, like the one at San Ygnacio, written in all capital letters, which read: "*EN PAZ Y LIBERTAD OBREMOS,*" or "MAY WE WORK IN PEACE AND LIBERTY." The *viga* inscription at the Rancho del Rincón read: "*RANCHO DE GUADALUPE JUNIO 24 DE 1867 SIRVIO A SU DUENO VIVANO GARCIA VIVA LA HORA DE DIOS VIVA LA PAZ,*" or "Rancho de Guadalupe June 24, 1867 served its owner Vivano Garcia, long live the hour of God, long live the peace." Another inscription read: "The peace of Jesus be with us. Dec. 3, 1871. San Ygnacio, Pray for us."[5] The heavy, hand-hewn *vigas* that have survived into the late twentieth century immediately capture the visitor's attention and still deliver their silent messages of faith and a frontier spirit.

The Tejanos used the strong *vigas* to support a flat, built-up roof for the stone homes or the *casas de sillar*. In some cases, thin roof stringers called *latas* were placed over the *vigas*. Most roofs were made of wider, hand-hewn boards called *tablas,* placed over the *vigas* to support a unique cement mixture of sand, lime, and small, round pebbles or pea gravel. This cement is called *chipichil,* variously spelled *tipichil;* in the late twentieth-century, it has become a staple covering for round stepping stones used in suburban patios. Tejanos developed this unique pebble cement for their nineteenth-century patios but also used it to cover the roof, laying it about eight inches thick. The *chipichil* roof was surrounded by the walls of the house, which extended about three feet higher than the flat roof and contained additional *troneras*. In times of attack, the residents could stand on the roof, behind the raised walls, and use it as a weapons platform overlooking the courtyard. *Chipichil* roofs also required minimal maintenance through the years and proved very efficient as an insulator and as a watershed.

In designing the *chipichil* roof, Tejano ranchers left it slightly graded in order to channel the scant rainwater down spouts called *canales* for collection and storage in a cistern of *sillar,* much like a rain barrel. Tejanos referred to the cistern as an *aljibe*—an old Arabic word which the Spaniards had learned from the Moors centuries earlier in Spain. Early Spaniards had transmitted

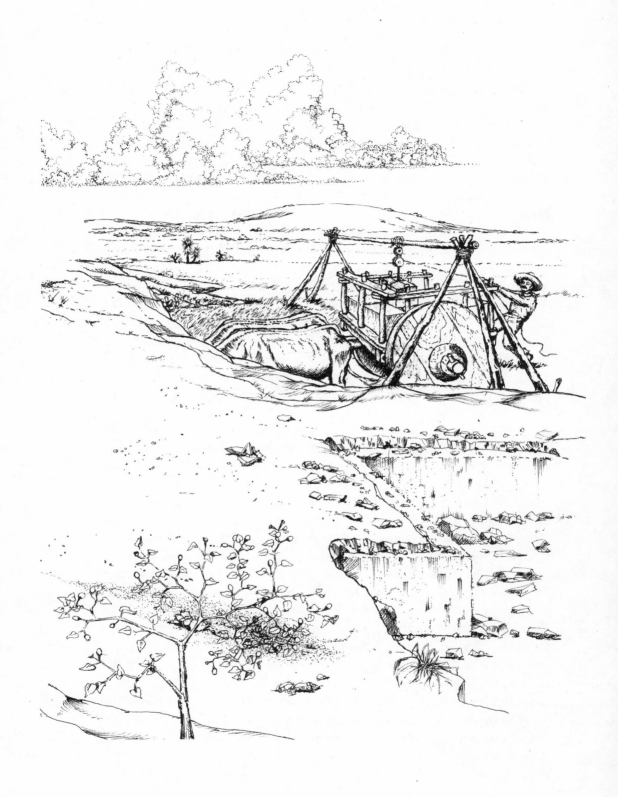

both the concept and the name for an *aljibe* to the New World, and Tejanos preserved it in their South Texas ranches. They called the stored dew and rainwater *llovediza* and considered it to be a very pure and precious commodity for medicinal use or other special purposes.

The *casa de sillar* was reportedly well insulated against cold in winter and against heat in the intense summers of South Texas. In the winter, the ranchers brought embers of mesquite, or preferably ebony, into the house to keep the interior warm. They built a fire outdoors to produce the embers, or *brazas,* then brought in one thick log that burned red-hot through the night. The thick *sillar* walls retained the ambient temperature for several days. Thus, the home's interior remained warm even after a cold front dropped the outside temperature radically. Of course, after a few weeks, the *sillar* absorbed and retained the chill, and the interior would remain cold even after the sun heated the outdoors. In general, however, the *sillar* served as a moderating medium.

A typical *sillar* house had no more than two windows, usually opposite each other along the two longer walls of the house. The windows were, of course, heavily guarded with thick, hand-hewn boards or shutters, and sometimes reinforced with wrought iron bars called *rejas.* In those *sillar* homes that endured into the twentieth century, the heavy mesquite beams in the window frames lasted as long as the stone or the *sillar* in the walls. Few of the early homes had glass windows, particularly in the early nineteenth century, although Adelaida Cuellar de Gutiérrez did write in her genealogy that her grandparents in the Zapata area used oxcarts to bring jerky, salt, and glass windows from Brownsville in the late 1800s.[6] However, most ranchers could not afford such luxury.

Tejanos had to depend on imported goods, often from Brownsville and Matamoros, for some of the finer furnishings in their ranch houses. They made their own heavy furniture of crude, hand-hewn mesquite or oak for the main room, or *sala.* Large families used a long table with equally long benches. And even the short benches or chairs rarely had a back rest. The most common bed was a plain *tarima* made of planks across a cot frame, with a mattress that rolled up during the day. Some families also used a softer cot of animal hide stretched over a wooden frame. Toward the late nineteenth century, wealthier Tejanos also used a canopy bed or a "Jenny Lind" of hardwood with a mattress. The mattresses were reportedly stuffed with shredded corn shucks, wool, or dry *paistle* (Spanish moss). These beds were covered with homemade quilts with ornamental edging of crochet or of a unique Tejano drawnwork. The nicer ranch homes were decorated with "silk draperies, marble top dressers, and tables."

Tejano families managed to appoint their homes with personal effects to make them quite comfortable. The men used rawhide and animal furs. One description of a Tejano bedroom said that "Deer, wild cat, and coyote skins took the place of rugs; mounted deer heads, powder horns and hunting guns hung from the walls." The men placed their rifles, pistols, and daggers on a shelf, while the women used a shelf for items like clothing or a crucifix. The Tejana women also used cupboards and shelves on the walls for crockery and utensils. But the Tejana's private corner was the altar, *el altarcito,* and historian Jovita González wrote:

> These home made ranch altars were the joy and pride of femenine [*sic*] art. At one end of the sala a sheet was hung to the wall; and on it were constructed with varicolored ribbons, red, yellow, orange and blue, arches and arcades that would have made an architect blush with envy. Sprays of cedar, oleander, and artificial flowers were pinned here and there making the already impossible arches more impossible still. Pictures of saints and angels formed a celestial host, and holy statues, some of wood and some of marble, were placed on the altar table.[7]

According to Fermina Guerra and to Emilia Schunior Ramirez, Tejanas always kept at least one trunk next to the bed to store their jewelry, finer clothing, and rolls of muslin. They used a thin cloth of soft cotton, called *manta,* for most items of clothing and underclothing and for other purposes around the house. According to one source, Tejanos bought "enormous" quantities of the unbleached cotton *manta* from Mexican merchants and used the material for bedsheets, pillowcases, and curtains as well.[8] The *manta,* like Tejano bedrooms, was plain, simple, and utilitarian. In the warm climate of South Texas, it was used much more than wool.

One of the most important rooms of a Tejano ranch house was not even in the house. It was the patio, which afforded the family the luxury of being simultaneously in the house and out-of-doors. The covered patio was almost always adjacent to the main house, connecting the *casa mayor* to a smaller house or *jacal* for the children or other relatives. Sometimes the kitchen was at the other end of the patio, enabling the women to use the patio's floor and shade as they cooked.

Emilia Schunior Ramirez indicated in her ranch history of Hidalgo County that ranch families used the patio from early morning until bedtime. They enjoyed its pleasant atmosphere for their meals, their siesta, and their late-night storytelling. They constructed the patio floor with a smooth, flat layer of *chipichil,* which in some cases extended beyond the area shaded by the patio roof. Indeed, some historical accounts tell of the families using the *chipichil-*covered floor for games, indicating that it covered a large part of the entire courtyard. The patio roof was constructed of four corner posts that supported a unique partial shading called a *ramada,* meaning branch entanglement. A *ramada* of bare mesquite branches provided just enough shade to break the burning rays of the sun in summer, but it was thin enough to allow warming rays in the winter. And it denied a nesting space to insects and rodents. The entire roof structure was called *el portal.* Many ranch homes also used this same structure as a front porch, which no doubt explains why the word *portal* in modern American Spanish refers to a front porch. For the outer walls of the patio, many ranch families used thick ebony logs, which they drove upright into the ground and placed side by side, reportedly "as solid as a stockade wall."

The patio had its own furniture—crude wooden benches and a patio table where family members could sit for a meal or a drink. For drinking water during the day, they kept a *tinaja* or clay jug, with a clay cup for a lid, hanging under the *portal* in a cradle of ropes, much as modern hanging plants are hung on a front porch. Tejanos customarily kept the *tinaja* covered with damp burlap which, according to one account, kept the water "incredibly cool" even on the hottest days. Another colorful item often hanging by a rope cradle under the *portal* was a flat, square cheese rack called a *zarzo,* covered with *manta* and kept hanging in the shade of the *portal.*[9] The *manta* kept the cheese dry and cool and protected it from insects and rodents.

Every member of the family placed items on the patio that they needed during the day. The men kept their saddles on the patio wall under the *ramada.* Indeed, some rancheros had a small corral next to the patio for their favorite horses. In one case, this required the ranch owner to walk his horse and the horse of a privileged overnight visitor right through the family patio. This was particularly convenient because he kept his tools and *reatas,* or ropes, on shelves on the facing wall of the house under the *portal.*

Although Jovita González vividly described the Tejano ranch house in a work of fiction, her words are instructive for a historical account as well. In her novel, *Caballero,* González listed the characteristic features of the ranch home of Don José Ramón:

> The armory with loopholes beside the gate, many bedrooms, dining room,
> kitchen, pantry, rooms for the cook and the housemaids, which could be
> turned into more bedrooms when the guests were many. On the other
> side another armory and his office, a huge *sala,* an *antesala,* a roofed porch,
> an open terrace like a platform. This filled half of the left side, leaving a
> square for the most important rooms, the outdoor living room called a
> patio. The palm tree was set beside the well, precious grape roots were
> brought to form an arbor. Tile [brought] by mule back across the moun-

tains from Puebla for the *sala* floor, sabine wood for the other rooms and the porch and terrace, from the Río Sabinas. A bell from the old ranch in Mexico which his father had brought from Spain, to swing in the high arch above the well, a sundial above the big gate. Seeds and flowers and vines, to make the patio a cool retreat in the summer. A long portico against the rooms, part of the gangway inside the gate roofed over, where saddles and other riding gear could be conveniently hung.[10]

One of the most distinctive features of the Tejano patio was the presence and aroma of flowering plants and vines, which covered the corner posts and the edge of the patio floor. Texas mountain laurel—a tall, verdant native shrub that covered much of the rockiest terrain in the brush country south of the Nueces—was a favorite plant around the patio of many Tejano ranches. It is especially beautiful in the spring, when it produces profuse clusters of purple flowers that from a distance look like grapes. The flowers, when agitated by the breeze, release a sweet perfume that made the plant a favorite courtship gift for young Tejanas. According to one historical account, "The lilac-like clusters of violet to purple flowers have a narcotic effect which accounts for the legend that if a love-struck youth presents them to his would-be *novia* the success of his suit is assured."[11] Tejanos called the plant *el frijolillo* because of its large, bright red beans. In addition to its evergreen leaves, spring flowers, and fragrance, the mountain laurel was a favorite around the patio because it required minimal care and watering.

Another favorite patio plant among nineteenth-century Tejanos was the wild olive, or *anacahuita,* which bloomed several times a year for weeks at a time. This small evergreen tree grows to no more than about fifteen feet in height, but its crown is covered with white bell-shaped blossoms about three inches in diameter, which drop to the ground overnight, covering the patio floor around the tree with white blossoms every morning. The tree's dark brown trunk becomes gnarled in irregular curves, making it an aesthetic specimen in the courtyard even when not in bloom. The blossoms yield after a few weeks to small, light-green olives that eventually ripen and drop to the ground. The olives' appeal to birds and animals helped to spread *anacahuita* seeds across the Tejano ranch frontier by the end of the century.

Another of the ubiquitous plants on the Tejano ranch patio was the white flowering jasmine, *el jazmin.* Jasmine not only produced a sweet aroma around the patio, but also served as the boutonniere of choice for those few rancheros who wore one in their lapels. Although such a luxury was rare on the ranching frontier, *jasmines en el ojal* or "jasmine in the lapel" was the mark of a *caballero* or gentleman. Tejana women also grew flowers in their ranch gardens, including Mexican salvia, the *azucena* or tuberose, the *rosa de Castilla* or rose of Castile, the *resedad* (a type of heliotrope), and the *alelí* stock. Tejanas appreciated these flowers as much for their fragrance as for their appearance. They also took advantage of the hardiness of these plants in the rugged South Texas terrain and climate.

Some of the most popular plants in the Tejano ranch garden had no flowers at all. The typical *hortaliza* or vegetable garden at a ranch house grew traditional Mexican staple crops of corn, beans, and *calabaza,* or squash, as well as a few rows of onions, garlic, chile peppers, cilantro, and watermelons. In addition to raising vegetables, Tejanos drew on their Mexican heritage to grow medicinal plants. They cultivated and regularly used herbs and shrubs for folk treatments in their daily ranch life. Vaqueros, for example, put the pungent leaves of the *amargoza* shrub in their boots to prevent athlete's foot. They used the bark of the *gobernadora* to make a tea for upset stomach. And ranch families gave priority to cultivating *manzanilla, albahacar, ruda, salvia, greta,* and *estafiate* in their patio gardens. Of all medicinal herbs, probably the most prolific was mint, or *yerba buena,* which grew in thick green clumps near the well or beside the rock walls of the *casa mayor.* Although the *yerba buena* and the *ruda* grow no radiant flowers, they were traditional favorites among Mexican medicinal herbs, not only for their use as teas, but also for the distinctive smell of freshness that they imparted to the home.[12]

At the other end of the patio, Tejanos customarily built a smaller house called a *jacal,* which was the rudimentary housing on the Tejano ranch frontier. In many ways, history has not been generous with the Mexican *jacal.* Those Anglo-American ranchers who lived in *jacales* in South Texas have not acknowledged borrowing this modest frontier home from the Mexican tradition, any more than they have acknowledged borrowing the livestock industry from the Tejanos. When non-Tejanos did happen to visit or to describe a *jacal,* their descriptions were usually disparaging. Indirectly, however, they provided strong testimony about the functionality of the *jacal,* for even the most condescending of these guests still preferred to sleep in the *jacal* rather than outside. One Catholic priest who passed through San Diego, Texas, in the early 1860s described the ranch *jacales* as "miserable structures" which had no floor or window screens but did have mosquitos and "other insects of a more repulsive type, which along with the stench of these miserable jacals, were almost unbearable." Despite his revulsion, however, the priest chose to sleep inside the *jacal* with his Tejano hosts.[13] To the Tejano, the *jacal* was not the housing of choice, either, but it sufficed on the ranch frontier until a more permanent home could be built. Indeed, Tejano families only slept in the *jacal,* spending their waking hours on the patio or outdoors.

The typical Tejano *jacal* could have a floor area as small as eight feet by twelve feet for a one-room structure, or as large as ten feet by twenty for a two-room structure. *Jacales* usually had only one or two small windows, a thatched roof, and a dirt floor that had been tamped hard and flat. To compress the floor, Tejanos cut a three-foot-long stump from a small mesquite tree, leaving part of a branch on the stump as a short handle to use while they tamped the moist dirt with the heavy stump until it was smooth and hard. Sometimes, they covered the floor with *chipichil.* The walls were a variation of the typical log cabin, except that the logs of a *jacal* were laid vertically, and were smaller in diameter because of the smaller trees in the region. The logs usually were covered with a cement or mud mixture to enhance the insulation value of the house.

To construct the walls of a *jacal,* Tejanos drove four corner posts called *horcones* about eighteen inches vertically into the ground. The *horcones* were forked at the top to hold the two main *vigas* or roof beams. Some Tejanos used vertical wall posts called *puntales,* also driven into the ground at intervals between the *horcones,* to provide additional strength for the mud mixture. They then laced long branches or slats of wood called *testeras* horizontally between the *puntales* and *horcones.* The *testeras* might be made of flexible willow, which could be intertwined through the *puntales,* or they might be of mesquite branches, called *leña.* Indeed, because of the wood used in the wall construction, a *jacal* was often called a *jacal de leña,* literally a "log cabin." One description of a *jacal* in Kenedy County indicates that the *testeras* were tied in place to the *puntales* with rawhide thongs that tightened when the moist cement mixture was applied to the wall.

After the wooden walls were erected, they were packed with a mortar of clay and lime to a thickness of ten to eighteen inches. Long-stemmed grass fiber was sometimes added to the mortar, producing a unique packing called *revoque.* The builder then whitewashed the outer surfaces of the walls with a lime and sand mixture that provided a protective coating.

Revoque used different kinds of long-stemmed grass fiber, depending on what was available in the region. Where the grass grew tall, Tejanos preferred to use the long-stemmed *zacaton* grass, which they also called *zacahuixtle.* *Zacahuixtle* is a Nahuatl or Aztec term for grass, indicating the *jacal*'s unique origins partly in Central Mexico and partly in the ancient Iberian Peninsula. Wherever possible, as they migrated northward into the ranching frontier, Tejanos systematically transplanted construction grasses specifically for *revoque* for thatch roofing. According to architecture historian Eugene George, they planted bull rushes called *tule* and reeds called *carrizo* in their *tinajas* or livestock ponds.[14] These, along with the native *zacahuixtle,* provided a depend-

able supply of long-stemmed grasses for wall construction and for thatched roof maintenance.

Because it was thatched, the *jacal* roof was gabled rather than flat. Tejanos called a gabled roof a *techo de dos aguas* or double watershed. To achieve the double pitch of the roof, a tall vertical post was erected between the two end *horcones* to hold a center ridgepole. These middle posts, according to anthropologist Joe S. Graham, were approximately twelve feet long, with a fork at the top end to hold the ridgepole of the roof. Tejanos then laid a series of mesquite rafters from the high ridgepole down to the *vigas* that lay along the top edge of the two long walls. On these rafters, they laid layers of bundled *zacaton* for the thatching and strapped the bundles of long grass to the rafters at intervals to give the roof strength. Although most Tejano ranchers made their thatched roofs of *tule* or *carrizo*, Emilia Schunior Ramirez indicates that the ranchers in the Rio Grande Valley also used palmetto and yucca leaves for the thatching.

With its whitewashed walls, dirt floor, thatched roof, and mesquite *ramada* for a front porch, the *jacal* must have been indeed an humble and picturesque abode for the modest Tejano ranch family. Yet visitors to the South Texas ranching frontier indicated that the Tejano families seemed content enough to live and to sleep in them. One report indicated that on some Tejano ranches,

the whole family slept in a one-room *jacal,* "or even groups of families lived in the one or two rooms." This and other reports always seemed to add that Tejanos gladly shared the meager space with family or visitors.[15]

As mentioned above, the Tejanos usually surrounded their ranch houses with a protective courtyard. Although some ranchers used stone walls to enclose the courtyards, most simply used a wooden fence or a hedgerow. Tejanos

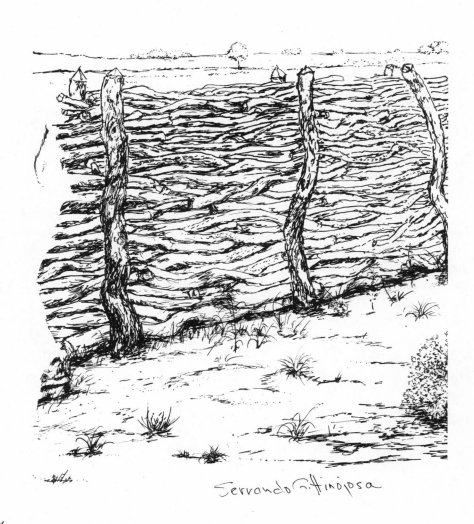

Servando G. Hinojosa

also used wooden fences extensively for their corrals. Indeed, their most common corral was the *corral de leña,* or "corral of wood," about five feet high. To build this distinctive structure, they laid horizontal mesquite logs one on the other, lengthwise between vertical posts which had been driven into the ground in pairs. To provide for lateral stability, Tejanos traditionally laid the fence sections in a zigzag pattern. The thin mesquite logs were jagged and uneven, which gave the fence its distinctive appearance. Some of these structures have endured into the late twentieth century and are commonly known as "Spanish fences." The *corral de leña* was limited in use because of the scarcity of logs, and it certainly did not approach the efficiency of later barb wire, but it served its basic purpose of security and livestock control. Moreover, it lent an extremely picturesque character to the courtyard around the *casa de sillar,* the patio, and the thatched-roof *jacal,* particularly as the old wooden fence developed its white patina and an overgrowth of vines and trees.

The distinctive trees of a Tejano ranch were peculiar to the region, partly because they had been propagated on the Tejano ranches. The *anacua,* for example, was a special tree among Tejano ranch families. Ironically, it has remained practically unknown to the general public and has usually been considered a "trash tree" by other Texans because of its growth characteristics. From a distance, the *anacua* looks similar to a common live oak tree, but it has multiple tree trunks—as many as five major trunks at its base—and dark green leaves that are sandpaper rough. Its evergreen foliage is very thick, yielding a complete shade on the ground beneath it. The leaf of the *anacua* incorporates a small pea-sized berry that falls and blankets the ground around the base of the tree, which provided a natural supply of nutritious chicken feed in the old ranch courtyard. The combination of berries, multiple trunks, and complete shade have made the *anacua* an unlikely shade tree for modern grass lawns, but for the Tejano ranch family, which had no grass lawns, it promised beauty, durability, and comforting shade.

Tejanos tended to identify the *anacua* as their own special tree, and it is, in fact, peculiar to the Tejano ranch lands. According to the Texas Forest Service, the "largest of its species in the United States" is located on the mission grounds of Nuestra Señora del Refugio in South Texas. And notwithstanding the modern public's lack of appreciation for it, the *anacua* is one of the few native flowering trees of Texas, turning white twice each year with what has been described as a "cloud of snowy, fragrant flower clusters."[16]

In fact, the rugged ranch country of South Texas is habitat to a number of flowering trees and shrubs, including the previously mentioned *anacahuita,* *frijolillo,* and *cenizo,* or sage, which bursts into purple bloom after a rain. The thorny *huisache* of South Texas is a fern-like small tree that also turns a rich yellow with fuzzy balls of tiny blossoms in the spring. Other native shrubs like the *guajillo* and the *granjeno* also turned the prairies white with their blossoms after a rain in the spring. The *guajillo* was a particular favorite with Tejano ranchers because its smooth branches had no thorns, and its thick green foliage provided their cattle with a substitute for grass in the worst of droughts. In a South Texas drought, the starving cattle often survived by eating only cactus and the leaves of the *guajillo* (plate 6). Some of the most successful Tejano ranchers were not ashamed to name their ranch estates El Granjeno or El Guajillo in honor of the prolific brush so characteristic of their region.

Tejano ranchers tended to cultivate their peculiar combination of trees and shrubs. For example, they transplanted large stands of the Texas sugarberry, which they called *palo blanco,* around their wells and corrals. The *palo blanco,* literally "white tree," is probably the tallest tree in the region. Tall stands of *palo blanco* gave the appearance of an oasis to many ranch homes otherwise surrounded only by miles of chaparral.[17] Where the ranchers built a courtyard, birds roosted on the fence, dropping the berries and seeds that eventually produced a virtual hedgerow of flowering shrubs or trees around the homestead. Decades after the corral itself had decayed to the ground, the hedgerow of *guajillo* or *anacua* would stand as the only sign that once a family had lived within a verdant, fragrant enclosure of familiar plant life.

Tejanos knew that water was the key to plants, trees, and life on the semiarid frontier of Texas, so their ranches tended to follow the contours of the watershed. And just as the *porción* land grants followed the edge of a stream, so ranch houses were placed near water wherever possible, bordering a creek or a gully to take advantage of the surface water or an underground water source like the springs at Los Ojuelos. The early Tejano settlers had brought their cultural knowledge of irrigation and water wells to the northern Spanish *frontera,* following systems that the Spaniards in ancient Spain had learned from the Moors of North Africa. Tejano ranchers demonstrated this knowledge in the canals, wells, and dams they built on their ranches in South Texas.

One of the most impressive structures on a Tejano ranch was the earthen dam, which Tejanos called a *presa.* Even in the late twentieth century, dams of this sort were still standing at such ranches as the Randado in modern Jim Hogg County and the Rancho de los Solís in present-day Duval County. Tejanos constructed the *presa,* typically about as long as one modern city block and about as high as a modern two-story suburban house, at a low spot on a creek or an arroyo, where it could capture runoff from the infrequent rains. After one or two heavy rains, the *presa* filled a reservoir large enough to water the livestock for several months.

Building the *presa* took months as ranch workers excavated the reservoir and packed the dirt into a dam. For digging, they used common hand tools like the pick and shovel, but for moving large amounts of earth, they used more specialized tools. For example, as the reservoir became deeper and the dam increased in height, the workers had to scale ladders and steep walkways to carry the dirt out in a burlap bundle on their backs, with a long strap looped around their forehead for additional support. This bundle, weighing at least forty pounds, was called a *mecapal*. For heavier loads, the workers used a large cowhide called a *guaripa,* tied at the four corners with ropes and pulled by a draft animal (horse or mule), to drag dirt out of the reservoir pit. The inner wall of the dam was then lined with *sillar* blocks to retard erosion. Within a few years, the dam was covered with a prolific growth of shrubs and trees, whose roots helped to reinforce the earthen structure. Ironically, the dense vegetation would also hide the *presas* from later archeological investigation, making them virtually indistinguishable from the surrounding chaparral.

The water well was another important water source. Tejanos used a small well for the family and a larger type of well for the livestock. The family well, called a *noria,* usually had a hand-drawn, wooden bucket called a *cubeta,* while the larger stock well was called a *noria con buque* because it incorporated a large rawhide tub called a *buque.* Both kinds of wells were lined with stone or with *sillar* blocks and had a wooden beam overhead to support a rope and pulley. The larger wells, of course, used heavy equipment; the heavy *buque,* for example, was tied to the saddle horn on a horse or mule to pull it out of the thirty-foot well. Ranch workers then poured the water into a long watering trough made of stone from which the livestock drank. On some ranches like the Santa Anita and Noria Cardeneña in present-day Hidalgo County, Tejano ranchers rotated their workers in shifts to drive the horse or mule back and forth, drawing and pouring water twenty-four hours a day.

Some stock wells incorporated a long pole rather than an overhead beam and pulley to extract the water. Using a heavy, vertical post as a fulcrum, workers balanced the long pole and used it as a lever, with a leather water bag on one end and a heavy, stone counterweight at the other end. Working around the clock, they dipped the bag into the well and lifted it out to pour water into a trough adjacent to the well. This method functioned only on wells that were shallow and wide enough for a short rope at the end of the pole to be dipped into the water at the bottom of the well. Tejano ranchers constructed such wells, approximately thirty feet long and three feet wide, in Willacy County and northern Hidalgo County, where the water table was quite shallow near the sand *médanos.* The workers at these wells also drew water day and night to supply the watering troughs for the large herds of cattle and horses.[18] The wells, large and small, made ranching possible in an otherwise formidable environment. With their cultural knowledge in the construction and production of wells, Tejano ranchers used the life-giving waters to support a viable community on the *frontera*.

Indeed, the Tejano ranch served not only the individual family members, but the entire community of ranchers throughout the region. In their remoteness from their home Villas del Norte, Tejano ranch families found it necessary to provide for their own education and religious needs. Thus, many of the ranches had their own school and chapel at the far end of the courtyard, and these were as important to the ranchers as their own houses. At La Noria Cardeneña, for example, the rancher Don Salvador Cárdenas was said to have built the schoolhouse "as soon as his home was completed."[19]

The ranch schools were not elaborate structures, nor were they elaborately equipped. The largest were no bigger than a typical *casa de sillar* and could be constructed of *sillar* blocks, stone, or of *revoque*. One schoolhouse at the Buena Vista Ranch near Laredo, for example, was made of stone and had a school bell, but according to education historian Guadalupe San Miguel, *rancho* schools were little more than "unsightly" *jacales* with dirt floors, only the crudest of furniture, very few books, and no blackboard. The school at Concepción Ranch in present-day Duval County, for example, had only "a table and some benches," and according to one traveler who had to spend the night there, the benches were narrow and the table "about two feet shorter" than he was.[20] Some schoolhouses occasionally substituted as chapels, storage sheds, or grocery stores.

Many of the larger ranches had their own general store or *comisaria* in the courtyard. These usually were no more than a simple, one-room *jacal* that served several ranches in the area with ranch supplies and other community services. The *comisarias* at El Peñascal and at Eulalia Tijerina's La Atravesada Ranch in present-day Kenedy County, for example, provided ranch supplies for a large group of ranches south of Corpus Christi after 1850. At La Becerra Ranch north of Laredo, the *comisaria* not only sold ranch supplies but also served as the mail collection and distribution point for surrounding ranches. Indeed, as the "curandero of the region," Don Casimiro, the ranch owner, even sold faith healing herbs and supplies there. A *comisaria* with an interesting variety of goods and services, of course, also attracted guests to the store as a social gathering place or simply out of curiosity. This was particularly true at larger ranches such as the Falcón Ranch in present-day Zapata County, where the presence of a *comisaria* and over one hundred residents in the early nineteenth century helped to attract five other business establishments as well.[21] These business centers also drew crowds during wedding fiestas and on religious feast days.

Religious events were set in the ranch chapel, or *la capilla*. Of all the community-oriented buildings on the Tejano ranch, the chapel had the loftiest appeal to Tejano ideals on the *frontera*. Even the chapel names spoke a strong message of the ranch families' hope and prayers. A chapel on the Rancho Blanco, on the Old Military Highway near present-day Brownsville, was named the Chapel of Our Lady of Visitation and was constructed of adobe bricks. The Santa Maria Ranch near present-day Edinburg had the old Santa Maria Chapel. Far to the west, the Tejano ranches across from the old Villa de Guerrero also had their chapels, including San Rafael Chapel at El Randado and another at El Rancho Lopeño.

In the San Diego area, the Tejano ranchers donated land and buildings for their chapels. The Perez family, for example, donated the largest chapel at San Diego, and families at the Peñitas Ranch, thirty-five miles to the south, set aside a building as their chapel. Both chapels served the surrounding ranches when the itinerant priests visited them as early as the 1850s. Another chapel in the San Diego region, at the Rancho La Concepción, was built around the 1870s.[22] As mentioned above, these chapels were simple *casas de sillar,* or in some cases, *jacales* with only a few crude benches, but the ranch families decorated them whenever a priest visited or when they celebrated a religious feast day, as detailed more thoroughly in chapter six.

Although many of the buildings in the courtyard were important at one time or another during the week, the kitchen was important every day. Located either next to the patio, or at the far end of the Tejano ranch house, the typical Tejano kitchen was detached and separated from the house by about ten to twelve feet. Usually, the kitchen consisted of nothing more than a fireplace or a stone chimney with a mantle or a shelf for cooking utensils. Tejanos constructed the chimney of *sillar,* stone *lajas,* or even *revoque.* In some homes, they used nothing more than a permanent campfire arrangement with a windbreak. In any case, few Tejanas on South Texas ranches had stoves.

The kitchen hearth was the eternal flame in the Tejano ranch household. The Tejana mother managed the fire and kept it burning day and night, rain or shine, although mostly in the form of a deep bed of embers or a smoldering ebony log. She kept the embers covered with a thin layer of dust during the night, and stoked them for the morning fire. Historical accounts indicate that Tejanas kept tortillas, a pot of *frijoles,* and a pot of coffee on the fire most of the day. The tortillas, beans, and coffee were almost as reliable as the fire itself in the Tejana's kitchen. Some Tejanas also baked bread in the outdoor oven or *horno,* which they preheated with coals until its walls were red hot. The corn or flour cakes baked quickly, providing bread for the entire week. And always present in the Tejana's kitchen were the traditional Mexican grinding stones— the *molcajete* and the *metate.*

The *molcajete* was the Mexican stone-age grinding mortar of lava rock. The rough stone surfaces easily ground the seeds, kernels, leaves, peppers, and powders that comprised the repertoire of the Tejana's spice rack. Rough, heavy, and ash-gray, the small stone was a shallow disk, traditionally about eight inches in diameter and about four inches high, which rested on three short legs. The *molcajete* was not complete without an egg-sized stone pestle for grinding. The hand-held pestle was called *la mano*, literally meaning "the hand." The *molcajete* and *mano* were so ubiquitous in the Mexican kitchen that they are the subject of a traditional Mexican riddle that asks: "I have three legs and only one hand. What am I?"

Along with the *molcajete*, the Tejana also used the longer, heavier *metate* for grinding bulk grains like corn. To use the volcanic ash *metate*, the Tejana either set it upon a stout table or simply knelt on both knees in front of the stone and let her rhythmic body movement literally push the ground corn meal off the end of the stone onto a collecting cloth. The shallow *metate* was about eighteen inches long and about twelve inches wide, with a companion stone, called a *metapal*, about nine inches long and three inches thick. The Tejana held the *metapal* in both hands and stroked its full length over the rough surface of the *metate*.

Other than the *molcajete*, the *metate*, and a complement of clay pots, the Tejana had only a few basic kitchen items such as a butcher knife, a cast-iron kettle, and a coffee pot. Some used only a heated, smooth-stone *laja* or flagstone to grill their daily corn tortillas, which were the staff of Tejano life on a ranch, but others cooked the tortillas on a flat piece of iron like a smooth grill, placed over the embers. Those who had copper or other metal vessels treasured them as heirlooms rather than using them over a bed of embers. The Cavazos family of present-day Mission, Texas, for example, had a copper kettle that had been brought from Spain in the early nineteenth century, but such luxuries were rare indeed on the Tejano ranching frontier.[23]

Most families ate their meals with plain flatware and very little silverware. The genius of the taco, of course, is that it required no dishes at all. When Frederick Law Olmsted, an Anglo-American traveler, encountered tacos while dining with a Tejano ranch family, he reported: "Our first difficulty was the absence of fork or spoon, but we soon learned from Woodland the secret of twisting a tortilla into a substitute, and disposed of a hearty meal." He added that the Tejano corn tortilla had an "excellent" taste which he deemed "decidedly superior to the southern corn 'pone.'"

For the most part, the Tejana had to depend on traditional recipes and her own resourcefulness to prepare the family meals. The Tejano ranch diet consisted of long weeks of monotonous simplicity interrupted by occasional feasts of rich, traditional delicacies. Typical daily fare consisted of four meals and a snack. Before work, Tejanos ate a light breakfast called *desayuno,* much like the European continental breakfast of sweet bread and coffee. They took their heavier *almuerzo* breakfast at midmorning, and a light lunch after noon. After a midafternoon siesta, they took a light *merienda* or snack of hot chocolate with a sweet bread such as *turcos*—a baked mince pie of spiced pork loin with cinnamon, sugar, nuts, and raisins. They took the *merienda* with visitors for a traditional chat to update themselves on the latest social events. And they ended their day with dinner late in the evening.

For their simple daily meal, Tejanos ate beans, dried meat, and tortillas with coffee or hot chocolate. They added rice, pecans, raisins, and a combination of meats from wild or domestic animals for variety. They commonly hunted such wild animals as deer, rabbit, javalina, dove, and quail to supplement their diet, making tamales or *chorizo* sausage from the muskier meats. Their domestic animals included turkey, chickens, cows, sheep, and goats. Although Tejanos had an abundance of cattle, the beef was difficult to preserve; therefore, they probably ate as much goat meat, or *cabrito,* as beef. Goats were much easier to slaughter, and the smaller amount of cabrito required much less preparation.

To preserve the beef, Tejanos salted and dried it into jerky, which they called *acecina,* referring to the very thin slices of beef cut from a large tenderloin. Or they simply called it *carne seca,* or dried meat. Probably more often than women, men prepared *acecina* in an elaborate—even meticulous—process. A vaquero working livestock out in the chaparral for several days prepared it and ate it daily. First, he heavily salted the strips, then hung them to dry in the sun. To expose the meat to the most sun and air and to prevent spots of moisture that might decay, he sometimes hung the strips on a taut length of sisal rope called a *soja,* stretched on a north-south axis. As the sun moved from east to west during the day, both sides of the meat received an equal amount of light. To prevent the two sides of the meat from touching, the vaquero separated them with a small stick, which resembled the crossbar in the letter "A." He took the meat down at the end of the day to protect it from mist or the morning dew. Then he tenderized the dried meat by pounding it with a wooden mallet on a tree stump. According to a visitor to the region, this process produced "beef sun-dried and cut up into slices which keep a long time."[24]

During the workday, vaqueros could enjoy an *acecina* while working, either chewing it much as modern Americans do chewing gum, or rolling it in a tortilla as a *taquito* and biting off pieces of it as they rode or walked along. Eating while working was a peculiarly Mexican way to eat a tortilla. Even those from other cultures and nationalities who have developed a taste for the Mexican *taquito* have rarely acquired the uniquely Mexican ability to eat one while riding, walking, or playing during the day.

Vaqueros did not make tortillas out in the chaparral; instead, they baked their own field bread, *pan de campo*. The bread was only slightly tougher and more dense than a devil's food cake, and, of course, it was salty rather than sweet. Vaqueros ate it with *acecina* and beans. According to an unpublished family history of the Hidalgo County de la Garza family, the vaqueros would "use leather chaps to knead dough in a sand depression to form a bowl. Then usually at the cattle water hole where fresh clay was shaped into a bowl where the ball-shaped dough was covered by clay also. A mesquite fire built on top of the buried dough resulted in a clay oven that hardened, cracked, and steamed as the bread expanded. The fresh bread was dusted clean and considered excellent companion with the hard tack of sun dried salted meat 'carne seca.'" Of course, the *pan de campo* was a traditional favorite with the entire ranch family at home as well as out in the field.

Tejano ranch families and vaqueros ate *acecina* on a daily basis and for all meals. For breakfast, they shredded the *acecinas* and mixed the salty shreds into a scrambled egg called *machacado con huevo*. Sometimes they added tortilla chips into the scrambled egg to produce *migas*. Often, they softened the meat in a bowl of hot beans for dinner. When the family had time for dinner at the house, the Tejana mother treated them to a hot stew of *acecinas* with a full complement of squash and spices, particularly hot peppers. Father Abbé Domenech recorded in his diary that he first ate *acecinas* mixed with cabrito, peppers, and other Mexican spices while visiting with a Tejano ranch family. His entry ended with the classic reaction to Mexican food: "After the first taste, I felt as if my throat was on fire." He described the appearance of the stew as "horrid" but evidently resigned himself and took the second bite. In spite of his reluctance, the priest and so many other immigrants to the Tejano ranch frontier were being converted to Mexican flavors in their diet.

Tejanos introduced the immigrants to tamales, enchiladas, tortillas, tostadas, nachos, and tacos, thus contributing to the spread of their Mexican culture along with the tasty dishes. For example, when the Tejana mother made tortillas, she also passed along an ancient tradition. Centuries earlier, the Mexicans of central Mexico had hybridized a starchy native plant called *teocentlí* into the sweet, juicy corn that spread to North America and the Old World, and the Tejana mother followed centuries-old methods in preparing it. She arose early in the morning to cut the kernels from the cob, then cooked them in lime water to remove the tough, yellow skin from the kernel. She took the resulting pulp, called *nixtamal*, and ground it on the *metate* to make cornmeal for tamales, enchiladas, tortillas, tostadas, nachos, and tacos.[25] A tortilla, then, was corn that had been cultivated, harvested, cooked in lime, ground, and hand patted onto a hot grill. The tortilla was simple, but it represented much more than just food. It was the stuff of Tejano life.

In addition to their simple daily meals, Tejanos had a rich tradition of seasonal delicacies and ranch specialties. Being on a livestock ranch, of course, provided a luxury of beef, cabrito, and mutton. But Tejanos also had specialized recipes for beef tongue, beef head, calf brain, beef tripe, and beef stomach. One of their favorite beef recipes was *barbacoa de cabeza,* or barbecued head of beef. For tamales, Tejanos baked an entire beef head overnight in a deep pit of mesquite *brazas* or embers, until the tender meat could be easily removed. This came to be known in English as "pit barbecue," and Anglo Americans quickly made the barbacoa an "American" dish. Anglo Americans were not so ready to accept another favorite Tejano dish, *menudo*—a soup made of a beef stomach that had been cleaned, diced, and cooked in hominy, chili powder, and other spices. But they were ready to include more beef in their diets, and it was, after all, the Tejano cattle that converted America from a pork- to a beef-eating nation by the end of the nineteenth century. The great change that would occur when ranch culture passed from Tejanos to Anglo Americans was not so much in the raising of cattle as in the marketing of beef.

Tejanos had their own reasons for the sometimes peculiar recipes they used. One was simply the abundance of particular food items. For example, they ate *nopal* or cactus because it was plentiful in the chaparral. The cactus leaf was about six inches in diameter and about one-half inch thick, and in the spring it produced a pear-shaped fruit about two inches long. Tejanos called the juicy, wine-colored fruit a *tuna* and sometimes made preserves with it. More importantly, they ate the green cactus leaf itself as a religious tradition during the Christian lenten season, when new cactus leaves were sprouting throughout the chaparral. The women of the ranch, guided by the family matriarch and the older women, selected the most tender of the new cactus leaves, called *nopalitos,* shaved the cactus spines with a sharp knife, and then cut the tender cactus leaves from the main plant. To avoid damaging the *nopalitos,* they carried the cactus in a basket, alternating layers of cactus with layers of tender mesquite leaves, moistened to keep the *nopalitos* turgid. The *nopalitos* were then cut into narrow strips and cooked with spiced meat or with egg. Although eating cactus was a deviation from the formal Roman Catholic Church teachings, Tejanos nevertheless considered their Aztec *nopalitos* to be an integral part of their own sacred tradition on the ranch frontier.

Another delicacy that Tejanos prepared for religious holidays was a sweet bread called *buñuelos.* This favorite dessert was literally a large tortilla of flour dough. At Christmas and New Year's, the Tejana mixed the flour with bacon fat, salt, and hot water, stretched the dough until it was rubbery, then rolled it "paper thin" and fried it in deep fat until it turned a crisp, rich brown outside but retained a touch of moisture inside. After sprinkling the hot *buñuelo* with powdered sugar and cinnamon, the Tejana served it with honey to anxious family and guests.[26] These sugary desserts were a seasonal treat, also occasionally served at feasts and weddings.

Tejanos also had a "wedding cookie" served either for wedding feasts or for Christmas desserts. They usually called the powdered shortbread by the descriptive term *pan de polvo,* literally "powder bread," but sometimes it was called *ojarasca.* These small sand tarts were made in heart shapes, as small round cookies, or in tiny, extremely fragile rings. The powdery cookies were made of pure lard, sugar, flour, and anise tea, baked or deep fried, then powdered with sugar and served with a hot chocolate drink spiced with fresh cinnamon sticks. Older Tejanos' accounts of this wedding dessert uniformly mention of the special emotional associations of the *ojarascas* because of the occasions on which they were traditionally served. There were traditions associated with the hot chocolate as well. According to an old Zapata County recipe, the hot chocolate was "whipped to a froth with a *molinillo,* the Mexican hand blender"; using this wooden cooking implement added an element of tradition and "the mother's touch" to the dessert.

The Mexican *piloncillo* candy always seemed to evoke a feeling of nostalgia in Tejano historical accounts because the sugar for it was taken from local sugar cane. In their history of Zapata County ranches, for example, Virgil N. Lott and Mercurio Martinez recalled that the resulting lump of "very sweet brown sugar in the shape of a cone" was traditionally served in the ranches of their area.[27] Twentieth-century youths of the region may prefer paper-wrapped candy from a vending machine for variety and taste, but like so many old ranch recipes, *piloncillo* seemed to offer an element of warmth along with its sweetness.

In that way, the *piloncillo* was representative of daily life on the Tejano ranch homestead. It lacked refinement and sophistication and probably was not suited to universal tastes. But it was based on the traditional folkways of the Spanish-Mexican *frontera,* and it was made to enjoy within the unity of the family, in the warmth of an old *casa de sillar.*

CHAPTER 3

Primos *and* Compadres
Across the Frontier

The family was central to life on the Tejano ranch, where people lived in large, extended families and thus developed different relationships than the predominantly nuclear families of the early Anglo-American frontier. A Puritan family in the late eighteenth century typically consisted of a father, a mother, and several children in a single household, but a typical Tejano ranch family of the time included great-grandparents, their married sons and daughters, grandchildren, and great-grandchildren, all in the same household, though not all in a single house. The Tejano family might occupy several small homes around the *casa mayor* of the grandparents, but the various units of the family depended on each other for their daily necessities.

Family was the basis for survival among Tejanos on the *frontera*. The Anglo Americans who came a hundred years later could depend on the U.S. Army, their government, access to American capital, and technology—including the windmill, barbed wire, and improved weapons—for support and profit on the frontier. By contrast, the original Tejano settlers had only the family to give strength to the colony and to conduct daily life on the ranch.

When Tejano pioneers first settled the Texas *frontera*, they came as whole families. Indeed, José de Escandón specifically sought strong families for his settlement expedition or *entrada* across the Rio Grande. He selected those who could demonstrate that they would survive on the rugged *frontera*. From the very beginning, then, strong family was essential to the Tejano experience.

As indicated in previous chapters, the major families of Escandon's five original Villas del Norte joined the move northward toward the Nueces. The cluster of ranches around San Diego belonged to the Perez, García, Canales, and other families from the old Villa of Mier, and the ranches in the Lower Rio Grande to the Ballí, Hinojosa, Guerra, and other principal families of Reynosa. Each of the other Villas del Norte had sent out its own large family groups to settle certain areas, and families on the *frontera* retained strong ties to their founding families back in the old Villas del Norte along the Rio Grande.

Through the early nineteenth century, these extended Tejano families populated their land grants with a network of ranches stretching from the Nueces River to Brownsville and from Corpus Christi to Laredo. Not only were the people on a particular ranch related through blood and marriage, but these large extended families also had strong relationships and common loyalties with families from other ranches through religious networks and confraternities, for example. The Tejano families collaborated economically as well; in building their ranching enterprises, they cooperated in such operations as branding and roundups. A cattle drive, for example, was possible because several Tejano ranchers contributed their cattle as the herd was being driven past their ranches on its way to market. Finally, the Tejano family networks laid a framework of trust and familiarity that could serve as a basis for political networks by the end of the nineteenth century.

One of the most representative examples of the extended Tejano family is the Garza family of the Rancho El Capote, located on the north bank of the Rio Grande on *Porción* Number 69 and *Porción* Number 70 in the jurisdiction of Reynosa. Originally granted by the Spanish crown to Juan José Hinojosa of Old Reynosa, the land passed into the hands of his heirs, who continued to live on it without subdividing its ownership until late in the nineteenth century, when it was under U.S. jurisdiction.

By the time of the U.S. census of 1880, Rancho El Capote had several houses, a store, a cemetery, and a chapel. It took the census enumerator two days, on June 17 and 18, 1880, to record the 47 nuclear families and 229 individual family members of the ranch that he scribbled in his notes as the "Capote Rancho." He had to travel around to the several clusters of homes spread across the ranch along the north bank of the Rio Grande. The handwritten census manuscript started with the names of fifty-five-year-old Guillermo Garza and his wife Leonarda but also recorded the several other names of Juan José Hinojosa's heirs, including Cavazos, Anaya, Cano, and Casares. The census also identified farmers, laborers, and many tradesmen, including a saddler, a general merchandiser, a silversmith, a shoemaker, a musician, a deputy inspector of hides and brands, and a carpenter.[1] Thus the census revealed not only the size of the ranch family, but also its self-sufficiency and interdependence.

As a result of the complexity of the extended families, Tejanos developed a highly specialized lexicon of terms for the myriad of cousins, in-laws, and second degrees of consanguinity. Likewise, they had unique terms for a brother- or sister-in-law that specified gender and level of consanguinity. Thus, while in English, the term "cousin" was used for any child of a person's aunt and uncle, in American Spanish, Tejanos drew a specific distinction between a male or female first cousin and a male or female second cousin. Indeed, their generic word for "cousin," *primo,* was used to mean simply "relative."

As Emilia Schunior Ramirez has written, each ranch in the Rio Grande Valley had its patriarch, who served his extended family: Silverio Solís of the Campacuas, Ramon Vela of the Chihuahua, José María Chapa of El Palo Blanco, Estevan Garza of El Rucio, Salvador Vela of El Veleño, Juan de la Viña of La Piedra, and John McAllen of the Santa Anita, among others.[2] It was one thing to be the father of a nuclear family, but quite another to have over one hundred men, women, and children looking to one man for their survival, education, entertainment, and livelihood on the remote ranching *frontera.*

As patriarch, the ranchero had unique privileges and responsibilities. He had unquestioned respect as the father to the families of his ranch community. He set the standards and enforced the values—sternly. The Tejano patriarch often worked with the vaqueros, although he usually did not perform the menial tasks. He provided planning, business decisions, and policy not only within his own family, but also to the larger community through a council of elders among the ranch owners. Guillermo Garza and Nestor Garza of El Capote, for example, served as the elders on that ranch complex and also as county commissioners, road commissioners, and ferry operators for early Edinburg and Hidalgo County. Likewise, Ramon and Manuel Cavazos were the elders on the Anacuitas Ranch, which later became the modern Texas city of Mercedes.

The patriarch of a large ranch had an image of grandeur, though not necessarily of wealth. He was the *don.* According to Tejano family legends, it was always a don who had led the advances on the *frontera.* For example, Don Hipolito García was known for having built the Randado as the largest, oldest working ranch in the region. Don Benito Ramirez built the stone fort at El Lopeño to defend his family against attack. And Don Salvador Cárdenas expanded education northward at his ranch, La Noria Cardeneña. A don was a gentleman, but he had his duty to the *frontera.*

Besides conducting ranch operations, the patriarch literally provided for the families on the ranch. He decided when an animal was to be slaughtered for distribution to all the families. The sharing of beef in this way established a special loyalty with the subordinate families. On one hand, they were grateful for the beef, but there was also a certain sense of entitlement as they, the workers of the ranch, accepted his provision. The patriarch personally bought the groceries and supplies for his ranch families. He, not the woman, went into Brownsville, Laredo, or Corpus Christi on horseback or in a cart to buy *la provisión*, whether it was flour, *manta*, or equipment. In town, he made purchases for his immediate family, for his workers, and for his neighbors. Along the way, he performed the social duties that were expected of someone with his patriarchal status. In the words of one contemporary visitor to South Texas: "When a ranchero is not either resting or amusing himself, he mounts his horse and canters over the plains and through the woods, to see his herds, to visit his friends, to buy provisions, or assist at a feast, a baptism, a marriage, or join in the fandango; but the ranchero never walks. Had he only half a mile to go, he does so on horseback."[3]

Indeed, the very appearance of the Tejano gentleman was of a man dressed to ride on horseback. The patriarch wore a Tejano hat, which today is called simply a "cowboy hat." It was smaller than the traditional Mexican sombrero, which was too large for riding in the wind, and larger than the old Spanish flat sombrero, which did not provide enough relief from the intense sun. Made of leather, the Tejano's hat was broad brimmed, lined with cloth, and curled up at the sides. The English word for the rim of a hat is "brim," but the Spanish word is *alas* or "wings," indicating the prominence of the Tejano hat brim. The crown was decorated with a gold chain or with several silver coins or decorative disks called *galones*. The hat accommodated about ten disks around the brim, leading to the English term "ten gallon hat." A vaquero wore leather pants and vest, but the elder Tejano wore a cloth jacket tailored in Reynosa, Matamoros, or Laredo and an embroidered white shirt beneath the jacket. His blue cloth trousers, with a side band of velvet down the leg, were split along the sides up to the hip, but buttoned or laced down to the knee. Below the knee, he revealed white embroidered drawers unfurled from the open split down to the ankle. His open trousers draped around his high-heeled, heavy leather boots. And his boots flashed large, silver, star-shaped spurs that, according to contemporaries, would literally "clank" with the slightest movement. The don wore a sash at his waist that was either bright red or white, although it was said of one Tejano that "a blue scarf of china crage encircles his waist."

If a Tejano gentleman presented a unique sight on foot, contemporary accounts indicate that he made an even more striking impression when mounted on horseback. During the Mexican War in 1846, U.S. Army officers reported that in their relentless cavalry attacks, Canales' rancheros of the Villas del Norte were "cruel" but were "superb" irregular cavalry, and even these uncomplimentary reports noted the Tejanos' colorful riding clothes, complete with bells and spurs. Another contemporary description of Tejanos in the Rio Grande Valley stated: "The majority of the rancheros were superbly mounted. Their saddles and bridles were mounted with silver, and two of the bridles were themselves of solid silver."[4]

Don Justo Guerra, patriarch of the San Pablo Ranch near Laredo, probably represented the upper extreme in colorful appearance and demeanor. Born in Castille, Spain, he reportedly wore fine clothes rather than leather chaps or a vest, sported a fresh boutonniere on his lapel every day, and carried a cane. Don Justo commanded his family and many servants as he went about the San Pablo, but he never worked. Indeed, it was said as a true compliment of this elder gentleman that "His hands were white and delicate, the fingers beautifully tapered like those of a woman." As a patriarch, Don Justo had more power over his ranch community than either the government or the church. Indeed, many of the smaller ranchers of the region looked up to him for leadership in ranching. The patriarch was, in the words of Professor Américo Paredes, "the final authority." And although Don Justo was above working with his own hands, he reared his two sons, Florencio and Carmen, to work along with the vaqueros and the servants on the ranch. He disciplined them to learn the values of sacrifice and dedication in the ownership of a ranch, and each son went on to become a ranch owner in his own right. Don Justo's adult sons freely deferred to the patriarch, sure in the knowledge that they would find justice and reward within the strict set of social rules.

In the legends of Tejano ranch life, the examples of such deference were legion. Roberto Villareal cites in his history of the vaqueros in Kenedy County that young ranch men could not—and did not—drink or smoke in the presence of their parents. On the ranch they drank only on holidays or as part of family fiestas, because public drinking was not tolerated in ranch family life. Although smoking was common in Tejano society, it had similar taboos in the presence of a patriarch. Professor Paredes cites an example of a "tough" Tejano who was casually sitting in a chair, smoking a cigarette with some other men in a room, but when he heard his father's voice approaching in the outer room, "The man straightened up in his chair, hurriedly threw his cigarette out the window, and fanned away the smoke with his hat."[5] As Paredes described the scene, this was not seen as subservience by the son, but as respect—even deference—to the patriarch.

While the Tejano patriarch commanded respect, the matriarch engendered love. She worked, she bore children, and she cared for the welfare of the entire ranch community. She had as long and arduous a workday as anyone on the ranch, and when she worked, she worked for the family. The mother set the social standards and religious values. Many of the schoolhouses and chapels, such as the one at El Randado, were built by Tejana matriarchs.

The Tejana matriarch made her primary sacrifice for the children of the ranch. She married when she was fifteen or sixteen years old and bore children for the better part of two decades. By the time her eldest were young parents and she was becoming a stately grandmother, she might well have given birth to over a dozen children, though she probably had lost at least one child to disease, to accident, or in the early years, to hostile American Indian attacks and kidnappings. Deeply religious, she led in organizing the religious ceremonies and festivals. She was the dignified leader of the wives and mothers of the ranch, the *doña* just as her husband was the don. But she had sacrificed her youth and her health in childbearing and in her arduous daily house chores.

From early morning to late night, the doña managed the mundane activities of the household. She personally engaged in the cooking, the sewing, caring for the garden and for small children and animals in the courtyard, and directing the several family members in their daily chores. Fermina Guerra described Doña Josefa, the matriarch of the Buena Vista Ranch near Laredo, as "mother, nurse, advisor, and companion," not only to her own family but also to the laborers and the neighboring ranch families as well. According to Guerra, Doña Josefa was "tall and robust, with refined, firm features that kept their grave handsomeness even in old age. She was quick in movement, active, intelligent, witty, and good humored. She was ready for a story or prayer, equally at home, at the fiesta, or in the sickroom."[6] But each day, she stoked the fire to awaken everybody else in the house with the morning coffee. In work, she was first, and at the dinner table, she was last.

Nor was the matriarch a tragic figure. While she supported the ranch family in time of tragedy, she was resilient. In fact, many Tejanas carried on with running the ranch after their husbands died. Mexican law—and later Texas law—gave women the right to community property, so a widow not only managed the assets but directed the scores of adult men and workers on her ranch. Indeed, some of the wealthiest ranchers on the *frontera* were women, such as Doña Rita Aldrete de San Miguel, who not only took over the ranch after her husband's death, but from the age of thirty until she had "snow-white hair," she also operated his freight business.[7]

Although she delivered loving care, the matriarch also demanded obedience and compliance with family rules. If some of those rules called for an adult Tejano to revere her above himself, she held firm. But her firmness, like her love, was for the family and its unity, which on the *frontera* meant survival. One of the strongest examples of a Tejano's respect for the matriarch involves Juan Nepomuceno Cortina, whose mother was the matriarch of El Rancho del Carmen, north of Brownsville in Cameron County. Cortina became a rebel to protest Anglo land acquisition in the county and fled south of the border, becoming a brigadier general in the Mexican army. When his mother crossed the Rio Grande to meet with him, he came to her to reconcile their differences. In the presence of his own army, General Cortina removed his cap and dropped to his knees, whereupon his mother ceremoniously slapped him once on each shoulder with his own riding crop. He then stood, embraced his mother, and asked her forgiveness.[8]

Other women on the ranch worked alongside the matriarch, though with less authority. They did all manner of work on the ranch from cooking and washing to baking bread in an outdoor *horno* or burning seashells there to produce lime. Most of the women's work was in and around the safety of the courtyard, but making lime could be dangerous: in the manuscripts of the 1850 census, architectural historian Eugene George discovered records of a ranch accident in which three census respondents—Guadalupe Córdova, his son, and his wife, María—were blinded by burning lime on the ranch.[9]

Making clothing and handicrafts occupied much of the Tejanas' time while the men were out in the chaparral working livestock. Tejanas carded wool, spun it, and wove cloth to make almost all of the family's clothing, using native dyes for color in most of their work clothes. Although they often bought dresses or a gentleman's suit from Brownsville, Matamoros, or Laredo, they made the clothes that they wore around the home: a chemise with a low front and a petticoat. The women were described as wearing a thin silk gown to go out of the home, and they covered themselves with a shawl or *rebozo* which, according to one description, "hangs about them in the most graceful folds." In making clothes, the women also used *manta*, linen, silk, and chambray, although "Kentucky jean" was popular for work clothes. They also sewed the leather vests that the vaqueros commonly wore.

In addition to making the clothing, Tejanas crocheted, embroidered, and did a unique type of drawnwork called *deshilado*, which was made "by cutting individual threads and pulling them from a piece of whole cloth to create an intricate design." Tejana women also did another type of cross-stitch on hemp cloth, called *canabá*, which reportedly was similar to needlepoint. They also used *manta* and other materials to make quilts, mattresses, and pillows for the household.[10]

The image of the Tejana that emerges is of a woman doing the chores of many persons, often simultaneously. A Tejana cooked a meal while she was washing and directing the family in other activities. For example, when the bishop made one of his rare visits to Buena Vista Ranch, Señora Panchita Alegría, a "respectable matron," decorated the courtyard all morning and directed the women and children to receive the bishop upon his arrival at the gate, while she rushed to finish preparing the meat for the feast. Señora Panchita was still cutting meat in the kitchen when the school bell rang, announcing the bishop's arrival in the courtyard. As he proceeded through the crowd in the courtyard, she rushed out at the last minute to kneel for his blessing. The bishop paused as he blessed her and facetiously asked her, "Are you going to kill me now?" According to the family story, Señora Panchita was startled to realize that she was crossing herself with one hand, and in the other, still firmly gripping the butcher knife that she had been using.[11]

Another image of the Tejana is of a fiercely independent pioneer who embodied all of the values of the Tejano family. Most Tejanas must have been brave and dedicated to endure the hardships of their remote homesteads, but one woman in ranch history stands out. Antonia Hinojosa was La Cautiva, or "The Captured Woman," for whom La Cautiva Ranch was named. She and her infant son had been captured by hostile American Indians while she was washing clothes on the Rio Grande. As she was being carried away from her son, she turned and saw him crying on the riverbank because the Indians had cut off his ears. For many years, she lived with the tribe, bearing a daughter, Carmen, for one of the braves. Carmen managed to escape and settled in Austin, Texas, and Antonia herself was eventually released in a prisoner exchange sponsored by the U.S. government. She took a homestead near Laredo and established her own ranch, where for years she stubbornly maintained her independence. She personally built her stone house by hauling stones from La Becerra Creek without the help of a single servant. Defending herself against bandits and hostile American Indians, she developed her ranch, even constructing a small *presa* and reservoir that were reportedly still visible in the late 1940s.

Antonia's daughter, Carmen, finally located her mother after several years of searching for her, and went to live with her at the ranch. Ashamed to learn of her Indian blood, however, Carmen returned to Austin after a brief stay, leaving her aging mother to continue her solitary struggle on the ranch. A few years later, Carmen received word of Antonia's impending death and immediately went to reconcile with her dying mother. Stopping to spend the night on a neighboring ranch only five miles from La Cautiva, she learned that Antonia had already died. Carmen became ill after reportedly "weeping uncontrollably" for several days at the neighbor's ranch and also died, never having reached La Cautiva. According to Fermina Guerra, "the two are buried side by side on the ranch of La Cautiva."[12] The families on the surrounding ranches repeated the story of La Cautiva among themselves, for it illustrated both the rigors that they endured and the essential qualities of family that they valued. The story of La Cautiva became part of their oral history, used for the same purposes as other family legends, stories, and fables: to teach the community's values to the young.

One of those values was work, and youths on a Tejano ranch began to work even in early childhood, when they helped around the house, fed the small animals, or carried water. By age ten or twelve, young men were expected to help the vaqueros with the livestock in the chaparral. Because of the demands and the structure of ranch life, children enjoyed independence early. Thus at the Palo Blanco Ranch, the Chapa sons had their own *jacal,* separated by the patio from the *casa mayor* of their parents. With virtually their own house, the popular boys could host their friends for unsupervised, overnight visits. But even as young adults, they were still expected to respect the family priorities.

Respect was the glue that reinforced Tejano family unity. All members were expected to respect their elders. For young men and women, that meant not only adults, but even older siblings. Young Tejanos and Tejanas addressed their father or mother in the third person, using the formal Spanish *usted,* or "thou," and their older brothers and sisters or older cousins with the same formality. Likewise, a young Tejano speaking to his older brother would address him in the third person, as "My Brother Juan," rather than simply by his first name.[13] The younger children were expected to show respect for all family members, and to listen silently while in the presence of adults. Though children were not spoiled, they were highly regarded in the Tejano family, as indicated by the care they received and by the birthrate reflected in nineteenth-century ranch censuses.

Childbirth and baptism were both highly ritualized activities in the Tejano ranch family. Some pregnant women were taken to a special place, such as a home in town or to a large ranch complex, if possible, to prepare for the birth. Many women of the region around Los Ojuelos went to that ranch, for example, for its natural springs during their convalescence. After giving birth, the mother remained in the care of a *partera* or midwife in the home for a specified *dieta,* or rest period of forty days. Doña Josefa Guerra of the Buena Vista Ranch moved into the family's town home in Laredo about one month before giving birth, and remained there for the entire *dieta.* Not all Tejanas were so fortunate as to have a home in town, of course.

The ranch women complied religiously with the procedures of the *dieta* when any mother gave birth on the ranch. A godmother or the aunts assumed the mother's duties during the *dieta,* caring for her family, cleaning house, and prohibiting her from doing regular chores, which they considered dangerous. They provided her with a special diet—thus the term *dieta*—feeding her only a fine corn meal called "*bastimento despicado.*" For this diet, the corn was soaked in lime water, as for tortillas, but the kernels were carefully cleaned to remove the yellow chaff, then sun dried and ground on a *metate* several times to produce a fine meal, which was then mixed with lard, water, anise, cinnamon, sugar, and salt. The *dieta* was not only highly selective, but ritualized as well. For example, for the entire time, the women of the ranch hung a lantern by the door and burned it continuously, reportedly "to petition God to protect the infant" before the newborn was baptized. Until then, he was considered at his most vulnerable, because he was not yet a baptized child of God.[14] Every child, they felt, should belong to God and to a family.

For those unfortunate children who had lost both parents, Tejanos systematically adopted them into one of the ranch families, and according to the nineteenth-century censuses, many ranch families included adopted children. As one history of the Tejano ranch community stated, "on the ranches of this frontier there were no orphans."[15] Although Tejanos established many institutions—ranch schools, chapels, missions, and even private high school academies in towns—there were no orphanages. Instead, any orphaned child was quickly incorporated into a family unit, which was considered the pillar of society.

The most impressive aspect of adoption among Tejano ranch families was that there was no social stigma on the adopted child. In fact, many children who still had both parents were evidently adopted informally by grandparents or by other members of the extended family who had the same last name. For children who were completely accepted within their own extended family, and who shared the same surname, adoption could be an almost insignificant fact. Whether related or not, the adopted children were treated the same as biological children of the Tejano ranch family. In the opinion of historians Virgil Lott and Mercurio Martinez, "It was and still is one of the most beautiful traits of these border people."[16] Indeed, in a principle later copied by the United States, the Mexican laws of Texas and Tamaulipas gave an adopted child all of the rights of any biological child in the family, to the point that an adopted male child, if he were the oldest in the family, could legally inherit the title to the land grant under the old principles of primogeniture.

Compadrazgo or godparenting was another strong social institution among Tejano ranch families. By serving as sponsors in a child's baptism, a Tejano couple became the child's godfather and godmother, or *padrino* and *madrina,*

respectively. They called their godson an *ahijado* and a goddaughter an *ahijada*.
Godparents sponsored not only the Christian baptism for newborns, but other
rituals or sacraments of the Catholic religion, including confirmation, first
communion, and marriage. In sponsoring the child's baptism, the godparents
usually arranged for a priest of the nearest town to visit the ranch to minister
the sacrament. Afterward, they assumed the role, literally as co-parents with a
shared responsibility to train the child in family and Christian values. Indeed,
the godparents could provide more effective parenting than even the biological parents in many sensitive situations.

The most significant effect of *compadrazgo* on the ranching frontier, however, was that it tended to link the extended families together in a broad community of loyalties. As a supplement to the formal sacraments, *compadrazgo*,
in the words of a priest, tended to "multiply these spiritual ties." Thus, while
the family name linked the several nuclear families within an extended family
on a ranch, *compadrazgo* linked several extended families together across the
entire ranching community. One history of *compadrazgo* among Tejano ranch
families stated that "all seem to be one another's compadres," linked by several
couples who had sponsored each other's children in one of the several sacraments which even the most remote Tejano ranch families received religiously.

Tejanos commonly practiced a unique relationship within the system of
compadrazgo: the relationship of a *compadre* and *comadre,* or co-father and co-
mother, respectively. When godparents became co-parents to their godchildren,
the birth parents commonly addressed them as *compadre* or *comadre.* But Tejanos
also established the unusual practice of declaring a close friend to be a *compadre*
or *comadre* in a relationship that involved no sacramental responsibilities for
the children. In such a case, two close Tejano friends asked a priest to bless
them together—two men or two women—in order to sanctify their close
friendship. As the two knelt together for the blessing, they exchanged a religious token, such as a medal or crucifix that the priest had blessed. These
relationships, known as *compadre* or *comadre de benedicción*—literally "blessed
compadre" or "blessed comadre"—were among the most sacred to the Tejano
ranch families.

Compadre relationships were so close a Tejano legend identified the shadows on the moon as two *compadres* who had quarreled and had been banished
there to show all others that God forbade disagreements between *compadres de
benedicción.* As one historian interpreted the legend's moral: "Friends may fuss
at one another, even brothers may have serious disagreements, but when one
has stood as godfather for another's child and has become a 'compadre' to the
parents, it is unthinkable that he should so forget his relationship as to quarrel
over anything whatsoever."

While Tejanos revered all of their family relationships, they reportedly considered the *compadres* to be among the most "beautiful relationships" of all. They spared no expense to sanctify a gift or an object of the relationship. One ranchero reportedly sold his favorite horse at the fair to buy dresses for the godmother of his children, his *comadre*.[17] As an expression of such feelings, Tejanos embraced the *compadres* of their family members as warmly as they did other members of their own extended family. As a result, a Tejano could presume hospitality in the home of his *compadre*, rather than waiting for an invitation. One account describes a visiting Tejano simply walking into his *compadre*'s home to sit at the family table "as if at home." Since Tejano terms of address expressed their respect for elders, a Tejano greeted an elder *compadre* by formally saying "*Buenos dias, Señor Compadre don Emanuelito*," in this case adding the diminutive suffix *-ito* to indicate endearment as well as respect.

The combination of extended families and the network of *compadrazgo* gave Tejano ranch families a uniquely homogenous community of *primos* and *compadres* that stretched virtually across South Texas. For example, one nine-teenth-century traveler described a trip that he took to Brownsville in the company of a Tejano patriarch, Don Eduardo. As Don Eduardo made his way through the chaparral, "He stopped at every rancho, and had a shake-hands with every one. He was full of anecdote and adventure. He was co-father to all the inhabitants of the frontiers."[18]

The unique combination of familial trust and economic interdependence allowed Tejano ranchers to engage in cooperative planning and operations, but this cooperation was not simply a capitalist imperative between ranch investors. It was a communal association, led formally by the patriarchs of several ranches in a region, which registered brands, conducted roundups, and settled their own disputes on the range. This association was a precursor for the cattlemen's association that Anglo-Americans would adopt, but for the Tejano patriarchs, it was as much a family organization as a business and, in Mexican Texas, sanctioned by law as well.

The patriarchal council met in the *casa mayor* of the most powerful regional patriarch. Sometimes the council convened for periodic functions, such as allocating a number of cattle to be slaughtered to provide fresh beef for the ranch families. Other times, the patriarchs met in response to a regional emergency, such as a flood or an attack by hostile American Indians.[19] But whether it was a formal association for economic planning or an informal organization to address the social welfare of the ranch families, the patriarchal council expanded the organizational structure of the Tejano ranching community, identifying and recognizing leadership and providing a functioning structure of trust and trained action. The council made decisions for a community of Tejanos who were highly trained by their culture to conduct their ranch operations, whether it was a roundup, a cattle drive, or a branding operation.

In fact, the planning, objectives, and informed leadership that the Tejano patriarchs provided served a vital function, not only making the Tejano ranch families confident in their decisions, but also reinforcing pride in their Tejano culture. Such cooperation was possible only in a community with well-defined ideology, according to historian Ranajit Guha.[20] Rural Tejanos had a strong communal sense of identity, of who they were; thus they referred to Anglos and to European immigrants in South Texas as *estranjeros,* or foreigners.

The decisions of the patriarchal council constituted what another historian, Edward Countryman, called their "political language." Both Countryman and Guha maintain that among rural folk groups who did not have access to political parties, to party conventions, or to official government positions, vital political discourse could be conducted through the family, the extended family, or quasi-religious loyalties. Thus, while the patriarchal councils could be seen as a group of old Tejanos lording over a humble rural society, they might also be seen as the political core of informed, intelligent leaders who used highly refined familial loyalties as an effective network for economic planning, resource allocation, and defense. Though they could not foresee it, they very likely also identified and trained the new generation of Tejano leaders who would have to help their community make the transition from a ranch environment to early twentieth-century urbanization.

CHAPTER 4

The Art and Skills of Tejano Life

W ork was central to life on the nineteenth-century Tejano ranches. Whether performing colorful roping and riding skills in the chaparral or cooking a meal at home, Tejanos and Tejanas worked all day, usually in family groups or work teams. Tejano ranch work was arduous, difficult, and dangerous, producing many anecdotes about accidents or death associated with ranch life. It was also colorful, and much of it was actually entertaining; the skills that Tejanos used for livestock handling are today viewed by millions as rodeo competition. But whether the work was pleasant or difficult, the way that Tejanos performed it reveals much about their work ethic. Work gave structure to their culture and, in many ways, reinforced the daily interdependence of family groups.

Tejana women not only worked closest to home, but closest to family as well. Immediately after a light breakfast or *desayuno,* the ranch women gathered at daybreak at the *presa* or a creek to do the day's laundry. On the Buena Vista Ranch near Laredo, they gathered at La Becerra Creek; in San Diego, at San Diego Creek; and of course, the Rio Grande provided miles of round river rocks that were ideal for washing clothes. It was work, but according to Emilia Schunior Ramirez, the women enjoyed a pleasant visit with relatives and neighbors over the morning's wash. And always they worked in groups.

Each day the young women of the ranch walked to the river to collect drinking water. The young Tejanas walked barefoot on a dirt trail to the river, each carrying a clay jug for water. Ramirez described it as a veritable morning stroll for these strong young women, and more than one contemporary description noted the graceful sway of the ambling water bearers. According to Ramirez, the women at Los Ebanos on the Rio Grande, south of present-day Edinburg, strolled "talking and laughing, with their empty clay pots—*tinajas,* they were called—held lightly at their waist. Half-way to the water's edge, on the sloping path, they would meet another group of young women, these with their *tinajas* full of water on their shoulder. They would pause to chat for half an hour or more, never seeming to tire of the burden of the water jug."[1]

Tejana women performed much of their work exposed to the elements, working in teams. To make lime, for example, they had to gather large baskets of scallops or mussels at the creek, then stack them in layers for the burning. They burned the shells for two days with patties of dried cow manure, which reduced the shells to "pure white lime," then sprinkled the stack with clear water to pulverize the shells. The process was completed when the women carried a 150-pound box of lime back to the ranch house. The women also had to coordinate with the men to make lye soap for household purposes. Whenever the men slaughtered a hog or a steer for meat, the women gathered the fat in large iron pots and, while the men were still butchering the animal, built a large fire to melt the fat. They poured some of the resulting tallow into candle molds and some of it into another large pot of boiling water, to begin making soap. They added a pint of lye to the mixture, then simmered it for four hours, poured it into molding boxes, and cut it into bars or large cakes while it was still warm. Of course, while they worked, the men and the women shared in lively discussions, and everyone enjoyed a bite to eat as the fresh meat was being butchered. If they were slaughtering a hog, the melted fat also produced tasty, rich cracklings, called *chicharrones.*

Another communal event for women on the ranch was the quilting bee. Like other frontier women, Tejana neighbors gathered at a ranch house for an evening of work and camaraderie. The hostess was responsible for the refreshments, carded the wool, and provided the wooden frame for stretching the patchwork quilt. Neighbors and relatives from the surrounding ranches arrived at the designated time, ready for the needlework or *punteo,* which ordinarily took a day or two to complete. The quilting bee was typical of the Tejana preference for group collaboration to accomplish tasks on the ranch.[2]

Vaqueros also worked in groups. Before going out into the chaparral, the South Texas vaquero dressed in his distinctive Tejano outfit: sombrero *galoneado,* boots and spurs, and *chaparreras,* or chaps. His chaps, which he stored hanging off the patio wall, were made of tanned leather, decorated with a fringe down the outer edges, but often were thick and stiff with age and exposure to sun and rain. Ranch hands used the same titles and work assignments that had been practiced in the Spanish ranching tradition since the early 1500s. The *caporal*, or leader of a ten-man team, called a *corrida*, would have to gather his vaqueros and the team's supplies so they all could spend several days in the chaparral. The *caporal* took his orders from the ranch foreman or *mayordomo* (plate 14).

A *corrida* would typically conduct a semiannual roundup of the herd to count the new lambs, calves, or foals for the spring branding and castration. After allowing the herd to fatten all summer, the *corrida* might round them up in the fall for slaughter or for a long cattle drive to market. The drive, called a *partida*, was often the culmination of the difficult roundup.

In preparation for the roundup, the vaqueros would gather supplies for a lengthy stay in the chaparral; typically they packed cooking utensils, green coffee, cornmeal, dried beef *acecinas*, baking soda called *salarete*, and chile peppers. According to one account, each vaquero also took his own supply of "black navy plug tobacco and prepared cornhusks for cigarette wrappers, lit by flint and steel each man carried," and vaqueros reportedly rolled and smoked their cigarettes at every opportunity.[3]

When the men of a *corrida* entered the chaparral with their supplies, their pack mules, and a small herd of decoy cattle, they established a *ranchito*, or campsite, where they would spend days or even weeks in the open. By all accounts, the work camp was austere; usually, it had no tent or roof whatsoever, no facilities for hygiene or grooming, and only a campfire for warmth (plate 1). The vaqueros had little need for the conveniences of home, however, for they ordinarily worked from 4 A.M. until dusk, every day of the week except Sunday afternoon. They prepared their own meals of *pan de campo, acecinas,* beans, corn, and chile peppers. They added any wild game they managed to kill during the day, commonly including turkey, dove, javalina, rabbit, or deer.

At work in the chaparral, the *corrida* divided into centuries-old roles and assignments by the traditional order of rank. The *caporal* was assisted by his *segundo*, or second in command, who helped manage the vaqueros on the *partida* or around the *ranchito*. The *segundo* also helped the *caporal* in managing the *cocinero*, or cook, and the *remuderos*, the younger workers, usually around age 10 to 14, who tended the spare horses while the vaqueros did the strenuous and hazardous work in the chaparral. According to Roberto Villareal's study of vaqueros on the Kenedy Ranch, the *remuderos* served as apprentices until they had demonstrated that they could be trusted with their own horses. Until then, they had to keep the *remuda*, or spare horse herd, fresh and ready for the vaqueros. On a hard work day, vaqueros would return to the *ranchito* every three or four hours for a fresh remount, and the *remudero* had to have the remount ready for a hasty exchange. A vaquero ordinarily used several horses in a single work day in the chaparral.

Vaqueros performed a variety of activities as they worked in the chaparral. Every ranch had its own champion vaquero in each of the cattle- or horse-handling skills, and these champions were the subject of ballads and fables on the chaparral. Tejanos took special pride in the ability to break in a *bronco,* or untamed mustang, and they reportedly tamed scores of wild horses on a mustang roundup. But sometimes they called on an expert, a *manzeador,* who specialized in "bronc busting," called *jinetear* in Tejano Spanish. In the San Antonio area, for example, the twelve Rodriguez boys and their father had reputations as expert *manzeadores* and reportedly performed the work on surrounding ranches for a minimal fee. Of course, there could be no medical attention if riders were injured while performing this work. Indeed, one ranch story told of a vaquero, Victor Suarez, who was thrown and violently stomped by a *bronco.* Suarez's life was saved only by the intervention of another vaquero. With broken ribs, Suarez remounted and broke the wild mustang (plate 7).

Another vaquero skill was cutting, called *cortar,* which involved separating a single animal from the herd.[4] Such skills were so spectacular that they are now popular events in rodeo entertainment, but Tejanos had no audiences and drew no applause as they performed the work from dawn to dusk. This is not to say, however, that they did not derive great pride in skillfully performing these feats as other vaqueros looked on. And, of course, they were sorely embarrassed or teased when they fumbled in such tasks. Indeed, any mistake in the chaparral could be dangerous as well as embarrassing (plate 3).

Roping, or *lasar,* was one of the most spectacular and aesthetic of the vaquero's skills, reaching its finest level of artistic skill in northern Mexico and South Texas in the nineteenth century. Because of the many demanding situations that arose while working with wild animals in the chaparral, a vaquero had to be versatile and highly skilled with a rope. The simplest method was to throw a rope from horseback over the neck of a running animal. But in the thickets of the chaparral, a vaquero often had to throw the rope while standing on foot within a confined area. In such cases, he needed to immobilize the animal by throwing his rope so as to loop two of its feet together. If the vaquero's rope looped only one hoof, a large steer or wild mustang could easily charge or drag him. But according to one study of Tejanos, these vaqueros rarely missed their target.

Vaquero roping skills were so intricate and so frequently used that Tejanos had highly specialized procedures and terms for them. Throwing a rope loop around a running animal's forelegs, for example, was called the *mangana,* while throwing the loop around the hind legs was called a *pial.* Sometimes two vaqueros would work as a team, roping an animal by the forehooves as well as the hind hooves. This technique was usually reserved for more aggressive animals such as bulls or stallions.

When throwing a rope from horseback, the vaquero had the advantage of his own horse's weight and the saddle horn to hold the roped animal. Using the saddle horn called a *cabeza de silla,* he executed a *dale vuelta,* meaning "give it a turn" because the vaquero would wrap his end of the rope with one turn or more around the saddle horn. This led to the modern English terms "Dolly Welter" for the saddle horn and "dally," from the Spanish *da-le,* which meant tying a single turn around the saddle horn. The *dale vuelta,* located at the center of gravity of the horse and rider, gave the vaquero a physical advantage, but even that involved danger. In order to prevent a sudden tug that might injure the roped animal, the vaquero wrapped the rope only two loops around the saddle horn, so the loose rope could spin out more gradually in an action called *chorrear.* However, the rope spinning around his saddle horn could move at such high velocity that the friction caused the saddle horn to smoke—and the vaquero could lose a finger as the rope quickly tightened around the saddle horn. In one incident near San Diego, Teófilo Salinas was working alone at night, roping a longhorn steer in the chaparral. When the rope tightened around the saddle horn, it pulled the entire saddle completely off his horse and sent Salinas tumbling into the air. Working alone at night, Salinas reportedly did not even bother to scream for help (plate 4).

Although the vaquero's rope work was hazardous and intense, it was also artistic in its performance. Indeed, vaqueros often displayed their skill and artistry deliberately, not to be ostentatious but simply to show their skill and pride. For example, in throwing the *mangana,* a vaquero would have to wait for the exact moment to throw the rope at the animal's moving hooves. While timing his throw, the waiting vaquero would twirl the large loop in interesting patterns, according to historian Kathleen Mullen Sands. "The roper swings the rope in ornate patterns, leaping through it from side to side, moving the loop up and down over his body, all the while counting so he will be in the right position to launch the rope when the mare gallops past him." She described another vaquero who tied the end of the rope around his waist while standing on foot to throw a *mangana a pie.* Having the rope tied around his waist gave him additional leverage, but it also demonstrated his confidence that he would not miss the throw at the animal's hooves. If he roped only one hoof, a large animal could easily drag him before he had time to untie the rope from his waist. Today, of course, these skills are popular primarily as staged performances.[5]

Even the ordinary work of the vaquero was an example par excellence of Tejano resourcefulness, skill, and teamwork, combined with a little romance.

This combination was most apparent in the Tejano roundup. To round up wild longhorns in the dense chaparral, vaqueros used natural materials, decoys, and singing. First they built a makeshift *corral de leña* and constructed "wings" of mesquite poles, about two hundred yards long, to funnel the stock into the corral. They set oak posts and a gate at the opening of the corral, using green cowhide straps as hinges, and placed a long, loose pole that slid across to shut the gate. Then they rode into the dense chaparral to drive the cattle toward the corral.

The vaqueros sent tame decoy cattle into the densest thickets to entice the wild longhorns out. As the decoys milled around the wild cattle, the vaqueros called out as if to imitate the "mooing" sound of the cattle, probably sounding more like "oomah" than "mooh." One fascinated Anglo who observed Tejanos in such a roundup described it as "a curious, coaxing, wordless song," which, for want of a better term, he labeled "the song of the brush." He said that "the song crept high and higher, and then sank low, gentle, soothing," until the cattle slowly followed the decoys out of the thicket and into the corral.[6] This was probably as close as Tejanos ever came to singing to the herds, but it may have provided a basis to the twentieth-century Hollywood portrayal of cowboys, strumming guitars and singing "Whoopie ti yi yo, Git along little dogie" to the cattle herds.

The romance of the roundup and *partida* did not extend to the long, monotonous hours of driving the cattle herd to market. The reality was that the vaqueros breathed dusty air and risked their lives on the long trail drives (plate 16). Roberto Villareal recorded an incident in which a vaquero named Martin Acuña was pulled under a swift current while crossing a river from Kenedy County to Kansas. The other vaqueros reported that "suddenly he and his horse disappeared under the water. The horse came up, but the vaquero did not." They followed the riverbank but could not rescue him; they later found Acuña's body downstream. One of the axioms of Tejano ranch life was that few people ever had the opportunity to learn to swim. In another incident on a cattle roundup, a longhorn bull struck the horse of Sam Smithwick, one of the best-known Tejano vaqueros in the San Diego area, knocking Smithwick and his horse to the ground. As the bull attacked Smithwick, Santiago Muñoz roped the bull and rammed his own horse into the bull's horns to save Smithwick's life. Ironically, Muñoz died shortly after the incident. Muñoz's wake was reportedly one of the few times that Smithwick was seen to weep openly in public (plate 5).[7]

Not all workers on the ranch were vaqueros. Others were servants or unskilled laborers who performed much of the same work as vaqueros but lacked some of the skills or social status on the ranch. Many were day workers, like the young men on the Hacienda Martineña near Laredo, who were hired from surrounding ranches by the French owner, Don Raymond Martin, to work as shepherds or as helpers to the vaqueros.

Some ranch workers, however, were more permanent employees who had been engaged by the ranch family for a number of years. In Mexican culture, these servants were considered peons; that is, they were in some way beholden to the ranch owner. The peon and his family lived on the ranch in a *jacal*, but he was not one of the people who owned the ranch in common. Instead, they received their food and housing from the *ranchero*, and perhaps even a small salary, in exchange for loyal service around the ranch. Their subordinate status gave them much the same behavior, and even the mannerisms, of a slave. But peons on a Tejano ranch were not slaves. They dressed much the same as vaqueros, ate with them, and enjoyed equality in their everyday life—something that would have been prohibited to slaves in the Old South at that time—but they definitely revealed the divided class structure on Tejano ranches.

In *El Rancho in South Texas,* Joe S. Graham succinctly reviewed the social class structure of nineteenth-century Tejano ranches, which maintained the class distinctions derived from the haciendas of the Spanish colonial period. There were clear social differences between the *ranchero*'s family and the peon families on the Tejano ranch. The peon looked to the Tejano *ranchero* not only as advisor and counselor, but also as a judge and a patron, or *patrón*. The peon and his family might plant a small garden around the *jacal,* but they looked mainly to the *patrón* for their food and supplies. Indeed, the hallmark of Mexican peonage was the ranch store, where the peon bought on credit and built up a permanent debt that would keep him beholden to the *ranchero.* The peon asked the *patrón* for permission to travel away from the ranch property, to summon a doctor, and even for his children to marry. In these cases, the *patrón* "would serve as the *portador* who would ask for the girl's hand in marriage for the peon's son."[8] According to Graham, this developed the peon's strong dependence on the *patrón,* and the custom of the *portador* would continue among Tejanos in South Texas throughout the twentieth century.

The living conditions of one group of peons, the shepherds, were particularly rugged. The typical shepherd, or *pastor,* needed no boots or even sandals, and he wore shortened trousers, a sombrero, and an open cloth vest. Anglo travelers who saw these peons often reported them to be barefoot and tattered. Like the vaqueros, the *pastores* slept under the stars or, at the very most, under a lean-to. However, they were more likely to work in pairs, if not in solitude, and they spent several weeks at a time tending their herd in the chaparral. Although they were considered insignificant, the *pastores* transmitted an untold wealth of skills and a centuries-old culture from the Iberian

Peninsula to South Texas. The legacy of the humble *pastor* is hardly known, much less acknowledged, by modern Texas sheep and goat ranchers.

Pastores were rarely literate, so their culture was almost entirely oral. Alone in the chaparral for weeks at a time, a *pastor* sang religious verses or recited prayers aloud to himself. Because they depended on oral communication, *pastores* were known for an uncanny ability to remember lyrics and poetry, usually in religious themes. One shepherd on a Tejano ranch in the Laredo area was known for singing one fourteen-stanza religious song:

> Dios de salve luna hermosa,
> Dios te salve luz del dia,
> Dios te salve sol y estrellas,
> Y Dios te salve Maria.

> *("God bless thee, beautiful moon,*
> *God bless thee, light of the day,*
> *God bless thee, sun and stars,*
> *And God hails Thee, O Mary.")*

The song of the *pastor* was indeed a simple one, but the sound of his music was an integral part of life on the Tejano ranch. In the evenings, ranch families could hear him singing, alone in the chaparral, as they put out their lanterns for the night. One wealthy *ranchero* who was dying in Laredo asked to be taken back to his ranch so that he could hear, one last time, the faint voice of the *pastor* softly singing his religious psalms across the tranquil chaparral.[9]

The Tejano ranch frontier was also home to a variety of other workers, many of them contractors who lived their lives on the frontier, providing vital services. For example, itinerant sheep shearers migrated to the ranches seasonally, cart drivers drove cart trains through with imported goods, and nearby merchants provided ferrying services and delivered drinking water. Of these independent workers, the sheep shearers were probably the most numerous and the most important to Tejano sheep ranching.

The sheep shearers were the aristocracy of the sheep industry workers. They traveled in troupes of twenty to sixty men, with at least one woman to cook for them. Before their work became mechanized, these proud troupes followed their leader or *capitán* as far away as New Mexico, Arizona, and the northern states of the Rocky Mountains. Tejano ranchers usually gathered their sheep herds twice a year, in April and in September, and one of the ranches hosted the shearers, known as *tasinques,* for sheep shearing, called *la trasquila.* (One ranch near San Diego was actually named Rancho La Trasquila, or Sheep Shearing Ranch.)

In his book, *North from Mexico,* Carey McWilliams includes a description from the 1860s of a sheep shearing troupe's arrival:

> The shearers would come in, a gay band of Mexicans on prancing horses, decked with wonderful silver-trimmed bridles made of rawhide or braided horsehair, and saddles with high horns, sweeping stirrups, and wide expanse of beautiful tooled leather. The men themselves were dressed in black broadcloth, ruffled white shirts, high-heeled boots, and high-crowned, wide sombreros which were trimmed with silver-braided bands, and held securely in place by a cord under the nose. They would come in, fifty or sixty strong, stake out their *caballos,* put away their finery, and appear in brown overalls, red bandanas on their heads, and live and work on the ranch for more than a month, so many were the sheep to be sheared.[10]

Once the work began, the shearers worked all day in teams, each team lined outside a holding pen where the sheep were kept for the shearing. The *tasinques* used spring-steel shears operated by hand to snip the wool from the bleating sheep. In the midst of the noisy, bustling operation, a *tasinque* would pull a sheep from the holding pen and drag it into a shearing pen, which was under a thatched-roof shed. With one quick movement, the shearer threw the sheep on its back, tied its hooves with a loop of a rawhide cord he carried in his belt, then rolled the sheep from side to side as he removed the fleece in a single piece. Afterward, he released the cord and chased the frightened sheep through the gate, out of the shearing pen. The *tasinque* would proudly shout *"Golpe,"* or "Bang," as the sheep hit the gate. He would then collect and pocket his token for the fleece, worth about two cents.

Other workers supported the *tasinque* as he rushed to shear an average of one hundred sheep each day. At noon, for example, his lunch was prepared by the troupe's cook, who was called "Madre." According to Fermina Guerra, the shearers called out "Madre-this and Madre-that" as they took their lunch, which was their only break throughout the entire the day. Another person who supported the busy *tasinque* was the *lanero,* or wool boy, who collected the shorn fleece and carried it to the packer, who stood inside a jute sack that hung in a vertical wooden frame, and tramped on the wool to pack it tightly in the sack. The packer then sewed the bale closed before loading it onto a cart for transport to Corpus Christi, Laredo, or other markets.[11] After a few weeks, the *tasinques* cashed in their tokens for silver dollars, broke camp, and rode out of the ranch with as much pageantry as they had displayed upon their arrival.

The people who hauled the bales of wool to market were the cart drivers, or *carreteros.* Although they did not live on the ranches, the *carreteros* were integral to the life and economy of the Tejano ranches. Like the *tasinques,* the *carreteros* were proud and highly skilled tradesmen whose work was more than simply their livelihood. It was their identity, distinguishing them from other Tejanos who lived on the ranches and from those with other trades or skills. One contemporary description of the *carreteros* indicated that they actually lived in the *carretas.* Frederick Law Olmsted, who saw some carts in 1850, wrote: "In these they live, on the road, as independently as in their own house." Another description of the carts around the Corpus Christi and San Diego area indicated that "Most of these carts had triple decks, with produce on one deck, goats and poultry on another, and the family on the other" and likewise noted that "It was their home."[12] *Carreteros* dressed differently from other Tejanos; they often traveled on the trails during the night; and their skills and unique knowledge had been passed down to them through generations of *carretero* families in northern Mexico since the conquest of the Aztec empire. Like the *tasinques,* the *carreteros* considered their trade much like a guild and were devoted to their trade.

Tejano *carreteros* dominated the cart trade in Texas and northern Mexico until the middle of the nineteenth century. They knew the trails from Chihuahua to Missouri, from Nacogdoches to El Paso, and from San Antonio to Mexico City, and they knew the Texas Indian tribes intimately. While the viceroy or the governor might be at war with hostile tribes or might attempt to cajole them with gift-giving ceremonies, the *carreteros* maintained their own relations to keep the cart trains moving through the Indian hunting grounds. When teamsters from the United States tried to penetrate the *carretero* trade routes, they found that without their own effective arrangements with the region's Indian tribes, the trails were unusable. Where the *carreteros* crossed a prairie unmolested, other teamsters encountered hostile American Indians. Where the *carreteros* served regular customers in the transport of wool, cotton, salt, and general merchandise, other teamsters found only scant freight business. Other teamsters might learn many of the skills, trails, or markets in the cart business of Texas, but it was still only a business to them. To the Tejano *carreteros,* it was a way of life, their family heritage, and their source of personal pride—as well as a hazardous business. Indeed, the only way that Anglo-American teamsters finally wrested the cart trade from Tejanos was through mass violence and ambush, in what came to be known as "The Cart War" of 1857. Legislators in Austin admitted to a "well known fact that a combination exists in the counties of Karnes and Goliad to murder peaceable, law-abiding, unoffending Mexican Cartmen—a fact notorious and undeniable." The legislators never stopped the murders, but they accurately stated that "the outrages perpetrated are a disgrace to us as a people—a stigma upon our character as a

State—a reproach to civilization."[13] Until the Anglo teamsters resorted to mass killing, however, Tejanos ruled the cart trade of Texas.

The *carreta* trade routes, of course, had been extended into Texas when it was the northernmost province of New Spain in the seventeenth century—and when Texas was most important for two main salt beds that helped to supply northern New Spain. One of the salt lakebeds was near El Paso; the other, in the heart of the Tejano ranching frontier near present-day Edinburg, was called El Sal del Rey, or The Royal Salt, because it, like all minerals on or beneath Spanish soil, was claimed by the Crown.

El Sal del Rey, once a natural depression in the sea floor, had been formed after the oceans receded from the Rio Grande delta, leaving a nine-hundred-acre dry lake of salt in layers up to four feet deep, with crystals that reportedly were ninety-eight percent pure. Originally, the Sal del Rey had been part of the royal grant to Captain Juan José Ballí, but for over a century, the carts had been coming north across the Rio Grande to scoop up the salt for distribution to the villages of northern New Spain. Just as the Spanish king had assumed the mineral to belong to *La Corona*—the Crown—so the Mexicans assumed that it belonged to *el pueblo*—the people—and made a regular practice of mining the salt for the Villas del Norte along the river. Tejano ranchers continued the practice. Indeed, later, when the price of salt increased from sixty-five cents a sack to twenty dollars during the U.S. Civil War, the Sal del Rey was considered "the most valuable piece of property in the state."[14] But whether it went to *La Corona*, to *el pueblo*, or to the Confederate States of America, the salt was gathered, transported, and marketed by the old *carreteros*, who by the 1860s had driven their old *carretas* under four flags in Texas.

The old *carreta*, the cart, was a curious combination of medieval invention and rudimentary technology. On the one hand, it represented one of the earliest uses of the wheel in the western hemisphere; on the other hand, the *carreteros* continually incorporated advances in axle, bearing, and wheel design. While improving the mechanical design, they also bred draft animals specifically for this arduous work. Modern Texas historians have generalized that in South Texas ranching, the Mexicans relied on traditional culture and the Anglos introduced technology. A review of the mechanical devices used by the *carreteros*, however, suggests that the differences in technology were more in degree than in category.

One of the most impressive parts of a *carreta*, according to contemporary accounts, was the wheel. Although the modern stereotype of the Mexican cart is of a small cart with small wheels, contemporary accounts consistently reported that the Tejano carts had wheels eight feet high, or in one report, "taller than a man." This large diameter allowed the solid wooden wheels to roll over rocks through undeveloped terrain. In the early nineteenth century, the entire cart was constructed of wood and even fastened with wooden pins. In his 1850 description, Olmsted stated that "The carts are always hewn of heavy wood, and are covered with white cotton, stretched over hoops," adding that the wheels were made "of hewn blocks of wood." Tejano cart makers preferred mesquite wood for the fellows and the main frame. As steel and technology improved after the 1850s, they began to add steel rims around spoked wheels and steel bearings that they obtained from New York.[15]

Before steel was readily available, however, Tejano *carreteros* made bearings from the wood of a *sabino,* or bald cypress, placing the bearing—that is, the inner lining of the wheel that encircled the axle—within a solid wheel made entirely of wood. *Sabino* wood bearings had a hard, smooth surface which the *carreteros* lubricated with grease or tallow, if available, or with the viscous fluid of the succulent cactus leaf so common in Texas. Thus they relied not only on tradition but on technological improvements and their own resourcefulness to transport a great variety of cargoes over long, hazardous routes. Indeed, the Tejano *carreteros* were using their *sabino* wood bearings at about the same time that Richard Arkwright, James Kay, and James Hargreaves were using little pieces of wood to make the flying shuttle and the spinning jenny in the United States. All of these contemporaries, whether they were improving American textile manufacturing or facilitating long-range cart transportation, were using basic technology.

The typical commercial cargoes transported along the Tejano frontier included longhorn hides, bales of cotton or wool, sacks of flour or salt, and construction materials. The *carreteros* also commonly carried consumer goods and provisions to the ranches, including *manta,* coffee beans, and sugar.[16] Across the Tejano ranching frontier, families depended greatly on the *carreteros* for ranch and personal goods, from heavy construction rocks and beams to finer articles for the home. Thus, while the *carreteros* were not actually ranch workers, they were closely integrated with life on the Tejano ranching frontier because they provided essential services to the families.

Many of the *carreteros* in Texas were actually ranch family members who joined the cart trains as drivers or workers. Conversely, some ranchers had, themselves, been cart drivers before they settled down to live on a Tejano ranch. Don Leonardo Arispe, for example, was a highly respected Tejano rancher of the San José Ranch near Laredo, who had selected his ranch site on La Becerra Creek while working as the chief muleteer for a cart train on the old San Antonio road during the Civil War. Other Tejano ranchers bred the animal herds and trained the mules and oxen for the *carreteros.*

Even without attacks from hostile American Indians or Anglo-American rivals, the *carretero* led a difficult and dangerous life. Not only did the cart trails traverse rugged terrain and hostile American Indian lands, but unlike the modern image of a Mexican riding on a cart, many *carreteros* actually walked alongside the carts, using a bullwhip to guide the oxen or mules. Thus, they were exposed to snakes, injury, or attack by mountain lions. Though highly skilled in balancing and tying the cargo, they also faced danger if their heavily laden equipment malfunctioned. One young Tejano, Erasmo Benavides of La Becerra Ranch, was killed on the cart trail from Laredo to San Antonio while repairing a broken cart wheel; his cart had been jacked up, but the equipment slipped and struck him. On the isolated trails of the chaparral, there was little hope of medical attention if a *carretero* was injured or became ill. The only comfort along the trail was a stopping place or *paraje*, where the *carreteros* could feed their animals and rest during the heat of the day. The few amenities of the *paraje* were shared in common by diverse travelers, from the *carreteros* to such military men as Lt. Col. Robert E. Lee and Gen. Antonio López de Santa Anna. For example, at El Paraje de la Parida, on a fork of the cart trail between San Antonio and Laredo, travelers regularly used the corrals and campsites for days or even weeks at a time when they needed to rest or make repairs while journeying through the chaparral.[17]

The *carreteros* were an essential background element of life on the Tejano ranching frontier. Though their trails were remote and isolated, their cart trains were the life blood of goods and supplies for ranch families. The *carreteros* seemed almost always present, reinforcing the network of lifelines across the chaparral. As one traveler journeying up the Rio Grande from Port Isabel observed in the mid-1800s, "You never fail to meet there a number of arrieros, or Mexican cart drivers, whose huge vehicles drawn by oxen are waiting for goods to be conveyed to Brownsville." Ranch family members might not even see the *carreteros* during the day, but their lives were full of reminders that the cart trains were never far away. Even as ranch families gathered on the patio to tell their stories at dusk or huddled in their *jacales* for a restful sleep, the faint echoing of the bullwhip, or *chicote*, sang out through the night, reminding them that the *carreteros* were somewhere out there, making tracks across the chaparral.[18]

For lighter transport, other Tejanos called *arrieros* drove trains of pack mules or burros. Though engaged in trade similar to the *carreteros,* the *arrieros* had their own distinct trade, accouterments, and skills. They traveled narrower trails through hilly terrain that was inaccessible even to the two-wheeled cart. They drove trains of thirty pack mules, each carrying up to 250 pounds for a distance of twenty-five to thirty miles per day between rest stops. The mules or burros transported some of the lighter items also carried by the carts, including hides, tallow, and salt. Sometimes longhorn hides were stacked so high on a burro that only the burro's feet and tail were visible beneath the load. The *arrieros* did not have to shoe or feed the mules and burros but allowed the animals to forage for themselves on the routes. Their trails, although narrow and difficult, extended to distant cities such as Santa Fe, Durango, Zacatecas, and Veracruz. Because of their lighter loads and trained animals, the *arrieros* fulfilled a specialized transportation function on the ranching frontier.

One type of local *arriero*, called an *aguador*, or waterer, transported water from the riverbank to the ranches. Each of his mules usually carried two water bags, made of goatskin or canvas, draped over its back. The *aguador*, often a boy, sometimes transported the water in a barrel mounted on a simple two-wheeled axle, pulled by the mule. The Abbé Domenech described one *aguador* in the Brownsville area, dressed "like the Lazzaroni of Naples" with open shirt exposing his chest, sleeves tucked up to the shoulders, cotton drawers turned up above the knees, and a straw hat of palm branches. He wore neither shoes nor sandals, nor a belt of any kind. Although a water boy presented a simple appearance, other long-distance *arrieros* were more mature.

Arrieros were very proud of their traditional knowledge and specialized skills. They sang ditties along the trail and called to their lead animals with the traditional *arriero*'s cry, "*Arre, arre.*" They were expert in tying a variety of knots to secure their loads, which rocked constantly from side to side on the mules' backs. A U.S. Army officer who watched two Tejano *arrieros* load their pack mules for the trail out of Corpus Christi observed in 1846: "Two Mexicans will load 25 mules in less time than my Co. will saddle each his own horse and get on parade." The *arrieros* were highly skilled, and their animals were well trained. Indeed, ranchers of the Villas del Norte specifically bred and trained asses and mules to be draft animals for the *arriero* trails. Santos Coy of Camargo was said to have employed five hundred men to breed and train over ten thousand mules for the *arriero* trade in South Texas and northern Mexico during this time. Like the *carreteros*, the *arrieros* were an important part of both transportation and ranch activity in South Texas.[19]

Although the cart and mule trains traversed difficult terrain, they both made extensive use of river crossings. There were no bridges across the Rio Grande or anywhere else in the Tejano ranching frontier until the late nineteenth century. When the rivers flooded, Tejanos avoided them except, perhaps, to ride a horse across the water. Otherwise they simply had to wait until the floodwaters subsided. When the water was down, they used a river ford called a *vado*, where the water was shallow and the river bottom would support the weight of a cart or animal. While the large *carretas* had to ford the river, lighter traffic or travelers used ferries operated by Tejanos at several *vados* along the

Rio Grande. Most ferries consisted simply of a shallow boat, hand-pulled by rope across the river. Some ferries, however, made use of a large, flat barge, also hand-pulled.

Where a *vado* offered a place to cross the river, ranch owners simply tolerated the traffic across their land. And where the *vado* seemed to need a ferry, called a *chalan,* it fell naturally to the ranch family to build and operate it. For example, the Garza family of El Capote Ranch, south of present-day Edinburg, operated El Capote Ferry. They were heirs to *Porción* Number 69 on the north bank of the Rio Grande, which the crown of Spain had granted to Juan José Hinojosa on October 22, 1767. Other well-known Rio Grande ranches also had ferries, including Rosario, Agua Negra, La Blanca, Granjeno, San Luis, Peñitas, and Las Cuevas. In addition to serving commercial freight, the *vados* provided the local Tejano ranch families with a pleasant location for camping along the cool waters of the river. Beatriz C. Izaquirre wrote in her family genealogy that her mother, Mrs. H. Cuellar, Sr. remembered gathering with the ranch family at the old *vado* across from Old Guerrero. There, the family would pass the hours of an afternoon watching the ferry workers or *chalaneros* slowly pulling the barge across the current of the river—a process that, according to Mrs. Cuellar, took thirty minutes.[20]

One of the largest and oldest ferries, of course, was the one at Los Ebanos, a few miles to the west of El Capote. This ferry across the Rio Grande had traditionally served the freighters from northern Mexico who collected salt at El Sal del Rey. At one time or another, the ferry at Los Ebanos served almost all of the historic persons and armies that operated in South Texas, including Robert E. Lee, Juan N. Cortina, John S. "Rip" Ford, and the army of General Zachary Taylor. After the U.S. Army established the Old Military Highway along the Rio Grande during the Mexican War, Los Ebanos and the other ferries became more regular in their service.

On September 2, 1852, the ferry at El Capote Ranch became the first officially licensed one in the newly established county of Hidalgo. The Garza family paid their license fee of one dollar per month, and then legally charged ranch traffic according to their regular rate schedule:

each person	*6 ¼¢*
each horse and rider	*12 ½¢*
each horse or mule	*6 ⅓¢*
each cart	*50¢*
each mule and cargo	*12 ½¢*
each barrel of freight	*6 ¼¢*
each goat, sheep, or hog	*2 ¢*

each wagon	*$1*
each yoke of oxen	*12 ½¢*
all cattle each	*6 ¼¢*

They also were licensed to operate a barge and a skiff, which Tejanos called an *esquifa*. The Garza family continued to operate the El Capote Ferry until just before the turn of the century.[21] In so doing, the family members of El Capote Ranch were like so many others who worked in collateral trades on the Tejano ranching frontier. Whether they operated a *carreta* or a *chalan*, they contributed vital goods and services to the Tejano ranch community.

But first and foremost, they were ranch families. Like the Garzas of El Capote, they lived and worked on their ancestral land grants. They were related to the other ranch families who utilized their special services. And they almost all worked as an extended community of the old Villas del Norte on the Rio Grande.

PLATES

Plate 1. The vaqueros spent days, even weeks, in the open, with no tent or roof.
Courtesy R. M. Beasley Estate

Plate 2. Tejano longhorn. *Courtesy R. M. Beasley Estate*

Plate 3. Any roping mistake could prove fatal on the chaparral. *Courtesy R. M. Beasley Estate*

Plate 4. Working alone at night, Teófilo Salinas did not even bother to scream for help. *Courtesy R. M. Beasley Estate*

Plate 5. Santiago Muñoz roped the bull and rammed his own horse into the bull's horns to save Sam Smithwick's life. *Courtesy R. M. Beasley Estate*

Plate 6. The starving cattle often survived by eating only cactus and the leaves of the *guajillo. Courtesy R. M. Beasley Estate*

Plate 7. With broken ribs, Victor Suarez remounted and broke the wild mustang.
Courtesy R. M. Beasley Estate

Plate 8. The mesteños were not only wild but aggressive. *Courtesy R. M. Beasley Estate*

Plate 9. Vaquero life on the *ranchito* was austere and unpredictable.
Courtesy R. M. Beasley Estate

Plate 10. Los Mesteños. *Courtesy R. M. Beasley Estate*

Plate 11. On La Trinidad Ranch, a wild mustang stood at the gravesite of Santos Moreno. *Courtesy R. M. Beasley Estate*

Plate 12. Back at the campsite, an angry bull found the cook, Pedro Valerio, an innocent victim. *Courtesy R. M. Beasley Estate*

Plate 13. Colon de la Garza. *Courtesy R. M. Beasley Estate*

Plate 14. A *caporal* leads his *corrida* on La Gloria Ranch near San Diego. *Courtesy R. M. Beasley Estate*

Plate 15. The stallion feigned injury and detained the vaqueros as his mares escaped over a hill. *Courtesy R. M. Beasley Estate*

Plate 16. The vaqueros breathed dusty air and risked their lives on the long trail drives. *Courtesy R. M. Beasley Estate*

Plate 17. Man often succumbed to nature in Tejano ranch life. *Courtesy R. M. Beasley Estate*

89

Plate 18. Colon de la Garza. *Courtesy R. M. Beasley Estate*

CHAPTER 5

Tejano Culture at Work and Play

I n 1985, music historian Manuel Peña wrote that Hispanics of early twentieth-century Texas played a peculiar style of music called "ranchera" be
cause it evoked their idyllic image of the old Tejano *ranchero*. The characteristics that Peña ascribed to this figure—"manliness, self-sufficiency, candor,
simplicity, sincerity, and patriotism, or mexicanismo"—have appeared not only
in music but in many other Tejano cultural traditions as well. Music has been
an important medium for communicating Tejanos' deepest values, but it was
not the only form available to articulate and preserve Tejano cultural unity.
On the Tejano ranches of the nineteenth century, families used formal education as another means of transmitting "mexicanismo" to their young. Religious and festive days throughout the year not only marked the people's daily
march across time, but also reinforced their shared beliefs. Their four-day
fiestas and dances in the private space of the ranches allowed them to assert
their competitive spirit, within strict guidelines of appropriate behavior, and
also provided cultural learning experiences. The oral tradition was strong as
well: whether in nursery rhymes for children or in the ghost stories told by
lamplight on the patio before bedtime, Tejanos used a variety of media to
articulate and to preserve their community. Consistently, the moral of their
stories was to value, to respect, and to have pride in their Tejano ranch community. By following a traditional set of daily observances and social rituals
and passing a rich heritage of music, story, and faith to their community, Tejano
ranch families elucidated their social order in a rapidly changing frontier.

Music was an important language for nineteenth-century Tejanos. It was private and non-threatening, especially because it was in their own language—Spanish. It illustrated in lyric terminology the highest ideals of the Tejano culture, and it could inspire pride, resistance, and self-sufficiency in even the youngest hearers. Among Tejanos of all ages, music reinforced their group consciousness.

It has been said of nineteenth-century Tejanos that "Many of the rancheros, without the slightest instruction in music, play the guitar or mandoline with no less taste than talent."[1] Some visitors misunderstood the value of the Tejano's music, thinking that it was only an idle tune to while away the hours. Quite the contrary, all classes of Tejanos on the ranch frontier used music constantly in their work and play. Vaqueros and *pastores,* for example, used music on a daily basis as they worked with cattle and sheep. Since many nineteenth-century Tejanos gained knowledge much more through hearing than through reading, music conveyed valuable information. To people oriented to the spoken word, music could transmit wisdom. A Tejano song, like a book, could be a storehouse of facts, transmitted across generations to teach the young.

Tejano men used group singing and ballads to reinforce their bonds of trust and security with one another. Tejano ballads drew upon the common words and objects of their daily ranch life, such as the guajillo, the mesquite tree, or the corral, and articulated the qualities Tejanos most valued. Thus, a ballad describing a wild, majestic mustang stallion that refused to be broken to the saddle used anthropomorphic adjectives to articulate the qualities that the men also admired in themselves.

One particular type of ballad, called a *corrido,* told a story. *Corridos* frequently related recent events, like the triumph of a Tejano hero or the daring deeds of a Robin Hood-like rebel. As soon as a *corrido* was composed, it was put to the chords of a guitar and transmitted from one ranch to the next, spreading quickly across the frontier. Once an event was memorialized in the lyrics of a *corrido,* it would be sung repeatedly by the ranch families until it became an integral part of their corporate knowledge. Through the singing of the *corridos,* the men shared a close, mutual friendship not often found in other societies. For example, during a fiesta on the Rancho de la Palma, the men staged horse races, then "walked about in large groups, arm in arm, singing to the accompaniment of the mandoline and the accordion." As they sang the lyrics of a *corrido,* the Tejanos recalled the stories that inspired them.[2]

One popular *corrido* praised an unbeatable race horse, El Prieto Pitoche, which belonged to Don Justo Guerra. Shortly after the horse won an eventful race on San Juan's Day, a *corrido* emerged, praising his triumph: *"En la carrera del Prieto. Un borlote se formo*" ("In the horse race of El Prieto. A Commotion arose"). In his study of the vaqueros of Kenedy County, Roberto Villareal translated another *corrido,* which praised an unbreakable horse called El Bohimio and taunted the unfortunate rider who failed to break him: "When Manuel mounted El Bohimio, / Who would have thought, / That in a few leaps, / Manuel was going to tumble." The final stanzas told of the vanquished vaquero making his exit on the road to "Las Labores," a neighboring ranch. Villareal explained that the *corrido* had a double meaning. "Las Labores" literally means "the farm fields," implying that the vanquished rider was cast away to become a lowly farm worker, rather than a proud vaquero.[3] Thus, through their singing, the proud Tejanos articulated the ideals that they pursued and the failures that they dreaded.

More than anything else, Tejano music articulated values, respect, and pride, preserving those idyllic virtues that music historian Manuel Peña identified. And if, as Peña asserted, twentieth-century Hispanics of Texas sought a worthwhile set of values in the old Tejano life of the ranching frontier, they certainly searched in a rich environment. For in almost all aspects of their daily life on the ranch, Tejanos cultivated pride in their culture.

Education, as much as any other activity, helped instill Tejano values in the young. Very few Tejanos were educated in Texas public schools during the nineteenth century, because the first public school in South Texas did not open until 1875, in Brownsville. Moreover, even after public education began in South Texas, students were instructed only in English, the Texas legislature having passed a series of English language laws between 1856 and 1870 that made English "the language of instruction for all public schools."[4] Thus the only education available to Tejanos was through their own private schools in town or on the ranches. Tejanos had little choice but to learn Mexican rather than United States history, and from Mexican teachers who taught them in Spanish. This may have given them pride in their "mexicanismo," but it continued to separate them from the rest of Texas.

A few parochial schools opened in South Texas, but their enrollment was very limited. In 1852, Presbyterian lay missionary Melinda Rankin, newly arrived from the East Coast, opened the Rio Grande Female Institute in Brownsville. The next year, Catholic nuns of the Ursuline convent opened the Incarnate Word private school, also in Brownsville, enrolling mostly Tejano students from five to eighteen years of age. In 1865, Saint Joseph's College, a Catholic school for boys, also opened in Brownsville. San Antonio also had parochial schools as early as 1860, when the Brothers of Mary and the Ursuline Sisters opened two schools intended primarily for children of "upper-class Texas Mexican families." The Ursuline Sisters also operated a parochial school in Laredo. All of these parochial schools together, however, enrolled only a few hundred students.

Tejano citizens in some South Texas cities also founded and maintained a few private schools. In San Antonio, for example, local residents of the barrio established their own Old Flores Street School in 1879, and later the South Pecos Street School. In 1897, the local Tejano population in Jim Hogg County established and funded the Colegio Altamira. This imposing structure, with one hundred students, mostly Tejano, operated in the rural community of Hebbronville until the 1930s. These private institutions provide evidence of the resourcefulness and support of the Tejano communities, but they were hardly adequate for the growing number of school-age Tejano children throughout South Texas. As Jovita González stated in her study of South Texas, wealthy Tejanos simply sent their children to Mexico for an education. Indeed, in 1848 the municipality of Mier alone enrolled over three thousand students in its public school system, which required public education.[5] This figure clearly revealed why Tejanos might look to their old Villas del Norte for education as well as for other cultural and family roots.

Mexican schools and private Tejano schools stressed the same patriotism that music historian Manuel Peña noted in the old Tejano idyllic culture. But it was a Mexican patriotism and pride, not patriotism toward the United States of America, and this further alienated Tejanos from the Anglo-American society that was quickly developing in the South Texas cities. Jovita González cited the example of a Hispanic county official in Edinburg in the early twentieth century, who had attended Tejano private schools and concluded: "We were wholly unprepared politically, educationally, and socially when the avalanche of Americans fell upon us. The fact that we received an entirely Mexican education, I am a product of the Colegio Altamirano in Hebbronville, made it difficult for us to understand American ideals."[6] And if the private schools in town nurtured "mexicanismo," so much more did the *rancho* schools, built and operated by Tejanos far from town.

On a Tejano ranch, the school was a source of pride, a sign of nobility. Don Salvador Cárdenas, patriarch of La Noria Cardeneña Ranch in Hidalgo County, built a schoolhouse as an integral part of his ranch near Edinburg. When asked what the building was, Cárdenas replied proudly, "A school—so my boy can go to school." Many of the larger Tejano ranches across the frontier had schoolhouses. The Concepción Ranch near San Diego, for example, had a *sillar* school building and a full-time schoolteacher on the ranch. In the Edinburg area, Don Juan de la Viña and Richard Marsh were the teachers for the ranch schools. The Buena Vista Ranch near Laredo had a permanent schoolteacher, Miss Ferron, although she lived fifty miles away, and a school building made of stone and reportedly graced with a school bell. The stone building that José Villareal built in 1851 on the San Ygnacio Ranch, near Zapata, boasted a sundial. Tejano ranchers like Cárdenas were proud of their schools, as part of their quest to bring knowledge and science to their ranch families. Some of the ranch schools even provided boarding for the boys who came from other ranches to attend school.

Schoolhouses were usually made of *sillar* or stone, although some were *jacales* with a thatched roof. The building was usually the size of a large house, with a rock or dirt floor, and was sparsely furnished with long, flat tables and backless benches. Jovita González indicated in her study of South Texas that the teachers at ranch schools often were from Mexico. Working without blackboards and using books from Mexico, the teachers taught Mexican history, ethics, basic reading, and etiquette. Writing in the 1930s, González, a teacher with a master's degree, was quite critical of the ranch schools' effectiveness in preparing Tejano children for modern American society.[7] It may be said without making a value judgement, however, that the prevalence of the ranch schools indicated the Tejanos' strong commitment to providing for their children's formal education, whether in parochial schools, private schools, or on the ranch. Tejanos certainly did more for their children's education than the government of Texas did before the turn of the century.

Nineteenth-century Tejanos on the ranching frontier, then, did not receive publicly funded, formal educations, although some received quality private educations. Many more Tejanos were taught and helped to preserve the region's rich culture and language through folk culture, passed from generation to generation. In his study of culture in South Texas, Américo Paredes indicates that Tejanos learned through a strong oral tradition. An integral part of that oral education process involved the Roman Catholic religion, which Tejanos learned by reciting fables, prayers, Christmas *pastorelas,* and verses, rather than by reading the Bible as Protestants did. A Catholic priest, Father Jaillet, noted that when he asked a Duval County Tejano rancher if he and his wife knew their prayers, the Tejano answered, "But, Padre, neither of us can read the Catechism, and we know only the Our Father and the Hail Mary; these we have taught our children." Though not highly literate in English or Spanish, Tejanos had a well-developed ability to recall and to recite the spoken word.

Another Catholic priest, the Abbé Domenech, was amazed when a Tejano peon near Brownsville gave a fine recitation of the medieval European mysteries "9000 miles from France." When he asked the peon how he could remember the entire "mystic verses," the peon responded, "It is my Christmas part." He explained to the priest that "for Christmas Eve we represent at the rancho the birth of Our Savior Jesus Christ, as is usual in a good many villages of Mexico. Three rancheros act the part of the 'wise men,' and I am one of them. Others are shepherds, and sing hymns to the accompaniment of the mandoline. The youngest and handsomest rancheros are the angels and intone the anthems." What amazed the priest even more was that in the *pastorelas*, a peon could be elevated to the role of a wise man.[8] The oral tradition indeed made "wise men" of even the humblest Tejanos.

Tejanos on the ranch frontier began at an early age to develop their ability for recall and oral recitation. Children's first words often came from nursery rhymes and fables that reinforced the Tejano place in their God's universe. And just as reciting poems and verses taught the children morals and etiquette, so the elders continued the practice, reciting the days of the almanac and the verses of the Bible. In either case, Tejanos borrowed wisdom from other nations and modified it to their culture. Many Tejano fables began with traditional knowledge from medieval Europe or the Aztec culture, subtly adapted to the ranch environment. The same was true of children's poems and fables, which offered a comforting alliteration that related directly to the daily sights and sounds of ranch life. Thus in the Tejano version of Uncle Remus, Br'er Rabbit became "Nano Conejito," and the Tar Baby was smeared with mesquite resin rather than tar. Likewise, Br'er Fox became a South Texas coyote named "Nano Coyotito," who inadvertently rubbed his eyelids with the spines from the "juicy and red tuna" of the prickly pear cactus. In another example, the South Texas plover's song was not "Kildee," but rather "*Tildio*," in Spanish.

> Tildio, Tildio! Tengo frio, tengo frio.
> ("*Kildee, Kildee! I'm cold, I'm cold.*")

In another poem, the South Texas *pastor*, minding his sheep, heard the mourning dove begging to be fed the *comas* berries of the *chaparral*, singing,

> Cu-u-cu, cu-u-cu! Cu-u-cu, cu-u-cu!
> Que quieres, pastor?
> Comer comas! Comer comas! Adios, pastor.
>
> ("*Coo-coo! Coo-coo!*
> *Shepherd, what do you want?*
> *To eat comas. Goodbye, Shepherd!*")

The fables interpreted the universe and reassured Tejano children that the world belonged to them. In her study of the Laredo ranches, Fermina Guerra captured this subtle message in the fable of the Milky Way, which Tejanos called the Caminito de Santo Santiago (the Little Road of Holy Saint James), "upon which travel the little ones who die in infancy where they are all kept together to play, and have all the food and things they need for a happy life. The cloudy part is the road, while the tiny stars are the children themselves." And as the children grew older, other fables continued to address their daily life and teach the lessons of life.

Older children played "El Florón," or "The Flower," in which they began to select from among the various professions in life. They sang,

> El Florón está en la mano, en la mano.
> Vamos a ver los talleres de la vida.
>
> *("The flower is in the hand, in the hand.*
> *Let us go see the occupations of life.")*

As they stood in line, as if going 'Round the Mulberry Bush, the children recited a series of poems about the *lavanderas, carpinteros,* and *albañiles,* or laundrywomen, carpenters, and brickmasons respectively. Besides this game, which helped to define gender roles and to identify the different Tejano professions, the children recited another fable that stressed the importance of securing a living. In the fable, the little chicken scratched at the ground with her feet because she had no hands. They recited,

> Una gallina con pollos, Carcaraqueaba y decía,
> Que tenía muchos hijitos, Y que con que los mantenía.
> Pues escarbaba con las patas, Porque manos no tenía.
>
> *("A hen with her chicks, Cackled and said,*
> *'I have too many children, And how shall I support them?'*
> *Well, she scratched with her feet, Because she had no hands.")*

The message was that in this world, a person must support the children even in the face of great difficulty. In another game, the verses of *"Una Pastora"* taught the Tejano children that "The Shepherdess" had to pay for sins she had committed. The game prescribed that she pay with a commensurate amount of penance.[9]

Respect played a meaningful part in the folk teachings of Tejanos on the ranches. A wondrous, celestial body like the moon inspired a classic tale about two *compadres* who quarreled, violating the expectation that *compadres* would always demonstrate loyalty to each other and never allow any argument to come between them. Tejanos said that the shadows on the moon were two *compadres* whose ranches were located on opposite banks of an arroyo and whose flocks of sheep always became mixed at the water, leading to confusion over ownership of the smaller, unbranded lambs. Forgetting the holy vows they had made over the religious medals that each of them wore on a small chain around his neck, the *compadres* argued over the flock of sheep, until God cast them up to the moon for violating their sacred vows and left them there as a nightly reminder for all to see.

Tejano children learned other lessons of respect for one another, for the natural environment, and for others in the community. They were told, for example, that children who were gratuitously cruel to small animals like the common horned toad, would be choked in their sleep by those animals, which would return during the night. They were taught to say "Ave María" to a visitor knocking at the door, or, if they were knocking at the door, they should answer "En Gracia." One of the most endearing habits that all Tejano children and adults learned was the salutation "*Jesús lo ayude*," or "Jesus bless you," when someone sneezes. This habit prevails even in a modern university classroom in South Texas, where a sneeze by the professor is likely to be answered with a resounding, unison "Bless you" by thirty-five otherwise quiet students.

In addition to learning values, Tejano children were taught good manners, appropriate behavior, and even hygiene habits through such folk lessons. Despite the arid conditions in which they worked and lived, Tejano parents encouraged their children to wash up before meals. As an example of the effectiveness of these lessons, an Anglo rancher, Walter Meek, after watching a group of Tejano *tasinques* sit down to lunch around the sheep corrals on Las Hermanitas Ranch near San Diego in the late nineteenth century, wrote in his diary: "I notice the Mexicans all wash their hands before eating." Meek admitted that he had always doubted that they washed their hands to eat, and implied that his current feeling of nausea might be due to the fact that his own hands needed washing as well.[10]

Even as they became adults, Tejanos continued their shared instructions for life. It was considered rude to visit during the siesta, which was usually between 1 and 4 P.M., during the heat of the day, but after their siesta, the ranch families visited over coffee and sweet bread. After another round of work, the adults gathered again to sit under a favorite tree or around the patio and smoke their cigarettes. During the early years of the nineteenth century, cigarettes had not yet become a habit with Anglo-Americans, but Tejanos in Texas would eventually introduce them to the habit.

In their leisure times, Tejanos told stories, sang ballads, and played formal games. The adult parlor games, called *juegos de estrado,* dealt with adult themes such as wealth, chance, and the social graces. They played El Caudal, literally "Wealth," by grasping a handkerchief from a player. They played La Baraquilla, a sort of flashcards game played with a handkerchief and based on the letters of the alphabet. There was a Tejano version of "Gossip," called El Secreto a Veces or "A Secret Spoken Aloud," in which they passed a whispered statement around the circle. As they played these games on the different ranches, the adults expanded their bonds of trust with neighbors from ranch to ranch. Indeed, many of the adult games were shared among *compadres* and *comadres,* enriching the bonds from family to family as well.

One of the most frequent pastimes in the evening was telling ghost stories around the fireplace. Tejano ghost stories followed a well-defined repertoire of classic themes. The most common themes were stories of treasure, of apparitions, and of classic characters like the Lechusa and La Llorona. The treasure story told of a local Tejano like Don Jesusito Serna of one of the Laredo ranches, who was riding across the chaparral at night and observed an eerie glow beside a bush. He returned the next day to dig at the spot and discovered forty gold Spanish coins, which he cashed in at the bank for a fortune.

One of the most common stories in South Texas was of the Lechusa, a witch who took the form of a screech owl, which Tejanos considered to be a bird of ill omen. During the day, she cast evil spells on innocent people, and at night, she screamed her ghastly sound and attacked lone travelers on the chaparral. The only defense against her was for a "good person" to recite the names of the four evangelists—"San Juan, San Lucas, San Marcos, y San Mateo." With that, the Lechusa would fall from the sky with a thud and, at her death, resume the form of the witch.[11] La Llorona was the classic Mexican tale of a woman who appeared in white along the river bank at night, weeping for her lost children.

Tejano ghost stories told about the Tejanos that the Texas Ranger "Rip" Ford had summarily executed on the old mesquite tree at the Santa Margarita Ranch, or about the old priest killed by hostile American Indians near the riverbank. Such stories, of course, contained the subtle themes that Tejanos were unjustly brutalized by the Anglo-American lawmen, or that innocent people could turn to their religious saints for protection from evil. In relating their stories night after night, Tejanos shared their common feelings of insecurity or persecution. By identifying the Texas Rangers as their common adversaries, they transmitted a shared critique of Anglo-American law and order in Texas. During the day, Tejanos might recite a rhyme like *"Rinche, Pinche, Cara de Chinche,"* or "Damned Ranger, Face of a Stink Bug." The lessons of their stories and rhymes were subtle but no less educational because of their informal methodology. Indeed, when presented by a trusted *compadre,* a story was a lesson for life.

Nature and the universe played a major role in the oral expressions of Tejanos. In one story, a black mustang stallion led his brood mares away from approaching vaqueros. The stallion feigned injury and detained the vaqueros as his mares escaped over a hill. As the vaqueros turned to him, he darted over the horizon to freedom. The story had an unfortunate ending, as the vaqueros later found the mustang dead, with a broken leg, presumably from stepping in a hole. Tejanos sang the praises of such a majestic animal (plate 15). Ranch people worked and lived among the mesquite trees and the guajillo. They cooked by fire in the morning, and told their stories under the stars at night. Even their favorite gathering place in the house was actually outdoors, on the patio. Not surprisingly, Tejanos expressed their appreciation of nature in games, songs, and poetry. In one rare instance, a listener was able to transcribe the words of an old Tejano near Brownsville even as he spoke, puffing gentle swirls of smoke from his cigarette and musing at the night:

> *. . . what a charming night it is!*
> *What sweet mellow temperature!*
> *What pure and balmy air! What silence in all nature!*
> *How this silence of night ravishes my soul!*
> *Do you hear the cry of the widow (long-tailed bird),*
> *As she flies along and flutters in the distance?*
> *Whither does she roam, poor bird?*
> *Why does she not sleep*
> *Beneath the thick broad shade of the ebony tree?*
> *Mystery of God!*
> *Do you see those myriads of stars*
> *Whose twinkling splendour lights the plains*
> *Like the timid doubtful twilight?*
> *And those majestic palm trees,*
> *Whose graceful branches gently poise themselves*
> *Against the clear blue sky,*
> *Seeming as if at night time they bear fruit of fire,*
> *Suspended from every branch?*
> *And those stars that fall and fade away,*
> *Leaving behind them*
> *A light narrow cascade of diamonds?*
> *Oh! how wonderful are the works of God!* [12]

There were no electronic tape recorders when these words were spoken in the 1860s, but in this transcription and translation, history preserved the words of at least one old Tejano gentleman. And his musings revealed the special feelings that a Tejano held for a balmy night under the palm trees along the Rio Grande. Nature was one of the most appreciated elements of Tejano life on the ranching frontier.

Because they had a well-developed sense of natural observation, Tejanos had another highly refined folk tradition, the almanac. Borrowing from their Spanish and Aztec predecessors, Tejano ranchers formally observed *la canícula,* the solstices and the phases of the moon, in their economic planning for the ranch's major operations. To determine the dates for planting, castrating animals, and harvesting, they used traditional folk calculation methods to determine the lunar phases. Their method for marking the lunar month, called "La de Epacta," involved calculating a complicated series of numbers assigned to the day's date, the number of months expired in the current year, and the number of days of the new moon. Though the calculation was very complicated, according to Fermina Guerra, "Everyone knew this number and all the almanacs carried it." When ranchers would greet each other on the chaparral, rather than using perfunctory greetings like "How's the weather?" they would exchange specific references to the current phase of the moon, *"La Edad de la Luna."* They also would ask *"Como estamos por cabañuelas?"* or "What month is it according to the *cabañuelas?"*—an even more complicated traditional almanac calculation for meteorological observations.

The Tejano tradition of the *cabañuelas* was modified from Spanish origins. The *cabañuelas* indicated the general forecast for the year, based on specific observations of the weather during the month of January. To make this calculation, Tejanos used the first day of January to forecast January weather patterns, the second day for February weather, and so on through the twelfth day of January for December weather. The thirteenth day of January also indicated December's weather, the fourteenth indicated November's, and so on in reverse order until the twenty-fourth of January. They then counted the twenty-fifth day of January again for January, the twenty-sixth for February, and so on to the thirtieth. On the last day of January, they then used each two hours of the day to indicate the weather for the twelve months.[13] While this folk tradition may be a quaint practice for accurate meteorological forecasting, it demonstrates the highly refined sense of recall and recitation in Tejano oral tradition. More significantly, it reveals that Tejanos did not simply while away their hours in idle storytelling, but used their highly specialized knowledge of meteorological observations, calculation methods, and traditional almanacs to provide structure in their life and to define the Tejano role in the order of the universe. From childhood through adulthood, Tejanos used rich music and folk traditions to articulate their ideals and their rules for Tejano ranch society. The folk culture was a practical reality, not simply entertainment.

When Tejanos wanted entertainment, they had a fiesta, an elaborate, four-day event staged in the privacy and remoteness of the ranch. The most important festive days for the ranch families were the Christmas holidays, Saint John's Day, Saint James' Day, Easter, and weddings. Each of these days had its own meaning, with unique customs, but all Tejano feast days also had many activities in common. For example, Christmas was the only season to stage the *posadas* commemorating the birth of Christ, but Tejanos held horse races at Christmas just as they did on all other feast days. A ranch dance was another feature of most feast days. But whatever the occasion for the fiesta, there was a prescribed pattern of activities that clearly defined it as a Tejano event. The ritualized activities of the dance reinforced their group consciousness. It was fun, but it was functional.

The most important feast day on the Tejano ranches was Christmas. Across the Tejano ranching frontier, the larger ranches cleared an area about the size of a modern city block in the main ranch enclosure, invited relatives and neighbors from the surrounding ranches, and set up booths and attractions. The guests stayed on the host ranch for the entire four-day festival, sharing accommodations and dining facilities. On El Sauz Ranch near Raymondville, for example, the fifteen families of the ranch brought an orchestra and built a large fire in the middle of the enclosure to keep the dancers warm in the evenings. Their games included bingo, horse racing, and gambling. A lantern called a *farol* burned at the door of the *casa mayor* from December 16 until midnight on December 24, called *La Noche Buena*, or the Holy Night.

An important Christmas custom was the *posadas*, which re-enacted the *Noche Buena*, as Joseph and Mary went from place to place, finding no room in the inn. Repeated several nights, from December 16 until the *Noche Buena*, the *posadas*, meaning "lodging," involved a procession of family members moving from house to house in the ranch enclosure. They would sing at the door, "Who will give us lodging?", and those in the houses would sing in reply: "We have no lodging, go elsewhere." At the last house, the "travelers" would be allowed in, and all the families would sing the rejoicing verses together as they proceeded into the "inn" for hot chocolate and *buñuelos*.

Another integral element of the Tejano Christmas celebration on the ranches was the *pastorelas* allegorical play, based on medieval European tradition and staged from 6 P.M. until midnight on the *Noche Buena*. Twenty-five to fifty players recited long verses, making it easily "the most elaborate" religious performance of the year. Even the audience would join in singing the play's tradi-

tional songs. The ranch family members, including the peons, each memorized their parts and played the traditional roles of the wise men, the twelve
shepherds, the devil, the angels—all in costume on an elaborate manger setting, which had the luxury of live sheep from the ranch. The players bore gifts
and tamales. Like the peon who became a wise man, the players were proud of
their roles in the *pastorelas* and rehearsed their lines throughout the year in
anticipation of the *Noche Buena*.

After the Christmas celebration ended, the ranch families continued their
holiday festivities with the New Year's Day celebration. The most important
element of New Year's was the dance, which brought multiple families together for a formal recognition of the *compadre* relationships. Amidst the games
and gift giving of the celebration, the main event was the "*Rifa de Compadres*,"
or the "*Compadres* Drawing." In the dance, the couples drew straws for all the
compadres to exchange dance partners. The dance allowed the many *compadres*
and *comadres* to formally recognize and to renew their special bonds of friendship. Afterward, they shared in the traditional refreshments of hot chocolate
and *buñuelos*.

Spring brought Easter festivities and the Feast of the Holy Cross, which
was commemorated on the first Sunday in May. The Easter feast included the
most elaborate mass celebrated on the ranch during the entire year. The priests
traveled many miles, circulating throughout the day to the largest ranches,
which were elaborately decorated for the event. That night, the ranch families
staged a dance that lasted literally until the following Tuesday morning. One
of the unique activities of the Easter celebration was the joviality of the young
boys and girls breaking egg shells called *cascarrones* over their heads. The
brightly colored *cascarrones* were filled with confetti, which scattered over the
hair and the best dresses of the girls. The confetti had sachet or perfume and
was considered to confer good luck. The señoritas also thought it might por-
tend that they could be married that year.[14]

The summer was marked by two major feast days, religious in their meaning and joyous in their commemoration. The Feast of Saint John, El Día de
San Juan, was on June 24, and the Feast of Saint James, El Día de Santiago, on
July 25. Both feast days were cause for great festivities on the ranches. Tejanos
held masses, followed ritual ceremonies, and staged three-day fiestas with horse
races and dances. San Juan, of course, was Saint John the Baptist. Tejanos
believed that on that day, the water in all the rivers and streams was blessed;
therefore they followed a ritual bathing in the streams. Tejanos of all ages
arose before sunrise and went out to the streams for their ritual bathing and
blessing.

El Día de San Juan was considered a special day for anyone named Juan,

Juana, or Juanita. On his patron saint's day, a boy named Juan would ride a horse through the ranch, holding a watermelon. In this game, *la corrida de la sandia,* the other boys would ride after him, trying to knock the watermelon out of his hands. The girls named Juana started the day being serenaded by the boys in the early hours of the morning. The boys set out at 1 A.M. and promenaded in a group on horseback until about 3 A.M., singing the traditional song *"Las Mañanitas,"* or "The Blessed Morning," and playing guitar at the windows of all the Juanas on the ranch. Even more sacred for the girls named Juana was the ritual cutting of their hair on their patron saint's day, also called El Día de las Juanas. Tejanos appreciated long hair in the women and believed that cutting it on that sacred day would make it grow more beautiful thereafter. The mothers cut the girls' hair by ritually chopping the ends with a hatchet or machete as the girl lay on her back with her hair draped over a wooden chopping block or across the door sill of the house.

On El Día de Santiago, boys named Santiago were selected to carry the watermelon for the traditional *corrida de la sandia.* Santiago, Saint James the Apostle, had been the patron saint of the Spanish people as they struggled against the Islamic invasion of Spain in the Middle Ages. Spaniards marching against the Moors in Spain carried the Cross of Santiago, which continued to hold a special meaning a thousand years later among Tejanos in South Texas. On El Día de Santiago, when Tejanos held a horse race, they used official judges and an official starter called "El Santiaguero," literally "the Santiago-er."

For a horse race, the men drew the starting line in the sand and the finish line with a handmade horsehair rope called a *cabresto.* Before the race, horse owners matched their horses to run against other horses in pairs. The matching was called *casar la carrera.* Then the owners declared the minimum amount for a bet on their horses and appointed three judges called *jueces veedores.* Each horse owner selected one judge, and they jointly agreed on the third, mutual judge who served as the Santiaguero. The Santiaguero was a respected person, trusted to settle any disputes. He started the race not by firing a gun, but by calling out *"Uno, dos, tres, Santiago Es"* or "One, two, three, Santiago." By many historical accounts, Tejanos bet large amounts on their horses in these events, and "A man's whole capital might be won or lost on a horse."[15] But the event was sanctioned under the holy day of Santiago, and therefore winners and losers respected the decision of the Santiaguero.

Religious feast days were not the only cause for festivals on the Tejano ranches. Indeed, by all accounts the most lively events were the wedding dances and celebrations. Although the wedding celebrations included horse races, booths, and other activities, the dance was the most significant event. When Manuel de los Santos and his bride were married on the San Pedro Ranch, for example, he paid for an orchestra of violins, drums, an accordion, and guitars for three days and nights.[16] Tejano fathers spared no expense to sponsor an elaborate wedding fiesta, selling their prize sheep and horses to pay for the orchestra or for dresses for their daughters. The matrons decorated the court-yard and patio dance floor with flowers and hung lanterns from the trees. The host family slaughtered a large cow or hog to provide an adequate supply of fresh meat for the four-day feast, and visitors from the surrounding towns and ranches contributed fruits, cookies, and liquor. All the activity around a dance stirred the ranch families to their highest point of merriment. The very name of the dance, *fandango,* sang a syncopated chord. Such a celebration dance was important, not only because it gave the hardworking ranch families a release from their daily duties, but also because it encompassed all the rules and ritual of the ranching community's social order.

The wedding dance started with the *convite,* the formal invitation, which in the Tejano ranch country was given on horseback. Forty or fifty young men and women of the wedding party rode across the chaparral at break-neck speed, stopping at neighboring ranches to sing songs and invite the neigh-bors. Starting out at dawn, wearing their finest dresses and vaquero outfits, they rode until midmorning, then returned in a cloud of dust to the gaily decorated courtyard of the host ranch. There, the orchestra members were already warming up their clarinets, violins, guitars, accordion, and the large ranch drum, the *tambora de rancho,* preparing to begin the days of dancing at around 10 A.M.

The *tambora de rancho* was a large drum, made of natural materials like goatskin drumheads with a wire rim, that was characteristically used for dances. According to Manuel Peña, Tejanos beat the drum loudly with "mallets whose tips were wrapped with cotton and covered with goatskin." Indeed, the loud drum began to beat even as the *convite* party was riding about the chaparral, "serving as a primitive sort of advertisement" to the surrounding ranches that the dance was about to start.[17]

The dance itself was a lively event that carried great significance for the ranch families, notwithstanding its somewhat rustic location. The dance was usually staged on a dirt patio in the courtyard, though at times it was held in the schoolhouse or on a prepared platform of wooden planks. Certain rules of etiquette had to be observed to demonstrate propriety in front of the ranch family's matrons, *las mujeres decentes* or literally "the decent ladies." All young ladies had to be chaperoned, and young men were not permitted to sing at the dance. Only the orchestra played for the dance, and they played only instru-mentals. These strict codes of behavior drew a strong distinction between the decent, private dances at a family ranch and the indecent barroom dances in town. Any drinking done at the wedding dance was communal and strictly limited to that occasion, using liquor that had been brought in from Mexico in sheepskin containers. This custom also distinguished celebratory liquor from the commercial distilled liquors that were sold and abused in the bars in town, and that Tejano ranch families regarded with the greatest disdain. Thus, even though the ranch dance was a feast and a frolic, Tejanos observed patterns and rules of behavior that made it not only their own unique form of entertainment, but an important element of their group cohesiveness. It was conducted in the privacy of their own space on the ranch, and it included only their own Tejano families.

Jovita González provided an inimitable description of a ranch dance and all its ritual meaning:

> The dirt floor was smoothed and sprinkled and packed with boards until it was as hard as a brick. Rough lumber benches were arranged in a square around the dance floor; a kerosene lantern furnished the only light. Every one, young or old, from the toothless old grandmother who smoked her shuck cigarette to the toddling baby, attended. Early in the evening the guests began to arrive in all their glory. . . . The dance began early. The mothers, rigid and silent, were the dragons who watched over their daughter's behavior. No decent, well-bred girl ever talked to her partner while dancing, and if she danced two sets in succession with the same partner she gave rise to scandal. By midnight the dancers were enveloped in a cloud of dust which from a distance appeared like a whirlwind and the dancers like spirits of the desert. At sunrise after playing *La Golondrina,* the orchestra and the dancers went home, not to sleep but to engage in their respective duties."[18]

It is unfortunate that historical research in Texas has totally ignored Tejano ranch entertainment while sometimes caricaturing the Tejano as a lazy drunk in a cantina. Tejano ranch life had its rich forms of entertainment in storytelling, feast day ceremonies, and strict rules of the ranch dances, and these entertainments were intended to reinforce the Tejano group consciousness. Their music, notwithstanding its entertaining character, was intended to transmit a message to the listener, portraying the Tejano as a proud, self-reliant, honest, hard-working mexicano. It can be no coincidence that one hundred years later, the old ranch family would emerge as the paragon of Tejano virtues, when their descendants immersed in an American educational system and society would search the roots of their own proud heritage.

CHAPTER 6

A Tejano Prayer

According to historian Timothy M. Matovina, religion was a major part of Tejano ethnicity—a way of demonstrating a distinct difference from the ever-growing number of Anglo Americans moving into South Texas. After 1836, Tejanos began to combine their religious ceremonies with other Mexican traditions specifically to emphasize their non-Anglo heritage. Their traditional Mexican patriotism, which already was emphasized in their private education in the ranch schools, was intentionally intertwined with their practice of Catholicism to further assert the equality of Mexican customs with Anglo American events such as the Fourth of July, Washington's Birthday, Thanksgiving, and later, Texas Independence Day. Then, according to Matovina, Tejanos infused religion into their education by teaching Catholic prayers and catechism in school.

In the elaborate, Mexican-inspired religious settings that they created, Tejanos venerated Europeanized images of the Virgin Mary to a lesser degree than they did statues of the Virgin of Guadalupe—the manifestation of the Virgin who was considered patroness of the Mexican nation. They refined their use of candles, flowers, and gun salutes as signs of their unique culture. Individually, Tejanos and Tejanas used medallions, crucifixes, and rosaries, and in their public religious ceremonies, they made use of ornate lamps, midnight mass, and youth processions.[1] Other Roman Catholic cultures also used some of these practices, but Tejanos actually began to emphasize their own rituals as an expression of resistance to the Anglo and European culture in Church ritual. But in their emphasis on these outward symbols, Tejanos were, in fact,

developing a tendency away from the Roman Catholic canon. This movement asserted the Tejano difference from Anglo Americans, and also proved
to be a great annoyance to the formal church hierarchy.

The Roman Catholic Church had been the traditional church of Tejanos
before 1836, but as the government of Texas fell increasingly under the control
Anglo Americans, the church began to replace the native clergy, with whom
Tejanos felt a traditional closeness, with priests of other nationalities. Jean
Marie Odin of Lyons, France, who was appointed bishop of the Texas diocese
at Galveston in 1839, began to introduce exclusively foreign priests—mostly
French—to South Texas through the order known as the Oblates of Mary. In
1847, he assigned the Rev. James Giraudon to Victoria, the Abbé Domenech
to Brownsville, and others to San Antonio and Nacogdoches. French missionaries would later move into South Texas as well. More than simply providing new ministers for the Tejano community, Odin sought "to suspend the
unworthy priests of San Antonio"—the native Tejano priests. Odin's Oblates
began to reinforce the official Roman Catholic canon by implementing new
practices and structures in their new diocese, which encompassed the Tejano
ranches.

Within a few years, Corpus Christi was designated as an official diocese for
South Texas. The religious orders of the Incarnate Word, the Brothers of Mary,
and the Ursuline Sisters soon joined the Oblates in developing new parishes,
churches, and academies in the South Texas cities. The Catholic parishes then
spread westward from Corpus Christi and northward from Brownsville into
the Tejano ranching frontier. By the 1860s, the priests began constructing missions and chapels throughout the diocese. They built the *sillar* La Lomita
Mission four miles west of present-day Mission, Texas, and collaborated with
the large Tejano ranch families in building a series of chapels at the larger
ranches. By the 1870s, the priests were able to travel on missionary circuits
throughout the ranching frontier, going from chapel to chapel to administer
their sacraments to the faithful. Soon, however, the Catholic priests found themselves struggling to retain their hold over Tejano religion.

The challenge came from Protestant churches that began to proselytize
within the traditional Catholic stronghold as soon as the Catholic Church
established its diocese in South Texas. In December 1849, the Rev. Daniel
Baker, a Presbyterian, arrived from Galveston and preached his first sermon in
Brownsville. He was later joined by two other Presbyterians, the Rev. Hiram
Chamberlain and Melinda Rankin, the latter a missionary schoolteacher who
arrived from New England and established her Rio Grande Female Institute
in Brownsville. A generation later, the Methodist Episcopal Church would
also challenge Catholicism when the Tejano families on El Capote Ranch

near Edinburg inaugurated their own Protestant congregation, El Capote Mission—recognized in 1878 as the first Protestant church in Hidalgo County, south of Edinburg.[2] With their congregational and diocesan structures established, the Protestant missionaries and foreign Catholic prelates launched their crusades for the soul of the Tejano ranch frontier.

Soon after the Rev. James Giraudon and the Rev. Abbé Domenech arrived in South Texas, the Rev. Peter Keralum and Fathers Verdet and Jaillet were sent from France as well. By 1850, seventeen French Oblate missionaries were regularly circulating among the Tejano ranches. Father Keralum, for example, traveled throughout his 100- by 150-mile jurisdiction—some 1,500 square miles of chaparral—visiting his 285 assigned ranches about four times per year. Father Jaillet also had a wide jurisdiction west of Corpus Christi, along the Nueces River, and regularly circulated to the Tejano ranches of San Diego, Las Conchas, La Trinidad, Santa Gertrudis, Petronilla, Concepción, La Rosita, Mendieta, Peñitas, Veleño, Lagarto, and Los Preseños.

The Presbyterian missionaries also traveled widely throughout South Texas. The Rev. Daniel Baker started at Brownsville and reportedly conducted services "at several ranches in the vicinity and continued as far as Rio Grande City." The Rev. Hiram Chamberlain, whose daughter Henrietta married the famous Anglo rancher Richard King, traveled northward from Brownsville toward Corpus Christi. Sumner Bacon operated near San Antonio, and Melinda Rankin conducted her missionary visits along the Rio Grande from Brownsville.

The life of a missionary was challenging. The Tejanos considered all of them to be "foreigners," and in many ways they were. Father Keralum, for example, was unfamiliar with the vast terrain on his solitary circuit and became lost while crisscrossing it on horseback. He died of hunger and exposure in the chaparral about forty miles from Brownsville, and according to regional historian Maurine Duncan, his body was not found until ten years after his disappearance; it was still surrounded by his sacred paraphernalia, his tattered saddle bags, and his horseless saddle. Even those priests who survived found that their circuits took them into an environment that was foreign to them. A priest journeying across the Tejano ranching frontier had to subsist on wild game, frijoles, dried *acecina*, corn tortillas, and hot spices. And at the end of a day of spicy foods, the well-meaning Tejanos would invite him to spend the night in their sacred little chapel—sleeping on the bench pews.

Though not always in agreement with the church hierarchy, Tejanos were still devout, and they anxiously awaited the arrival of the missionaries to sanctify their wedding vows, to baptize children, to conduct mass, and to bless the variety of religious objects of the *compadrazgo* vows. As soon as the missionary arrived on the ranch, he was surrounded by children and adults, each holding out medals, crosses, images, and rosaries to be blessed with his holy water. *Compadres* came before him and asked to be blessed, along with the medals that they exchanged. Parents held their children up to be baptized, often asking the missionary to stand as the *padrino*. Indeed, one priest described his own involuntary entanglement in the rush of the ceremonies at the ranch. "For each blessing," he said, "the owner of the article chose a godfather and godmother who, with himself and the priest, became *Compadre* and *Comadre de benedicción,* so that in about an hour I was related to the entire rancho."[3] Notwithstanding the joyful reception, however, the priests were only visitors—foreigners in Tejano ranch life.

The missionaries themselves freely articulated their sense of alienation from Tejanos. Bishop Odin's new Roman Catholic clergy harshly rejected Tejano rituals that deviated from the formal Church canon, according to Timothy Matovina's history of *Tejano Religion and Ethnicity*. They disdained the Tejano practice of kneeling long before reaching the altar—a practice that was more Mexican than Catholic. A Catholic nun made it clear that these were significant annoyances: "These incidents may seem to be minor events, not noticed by the general congregation," she said, adding that "Anyone thinking thus is very much mistaken." And if the Catholic priests rejected some Catholic Tejano beliefs, the incompatibility with Protestant missionaries was even greater. Furthermore, none of the missionaries, French or Anglo, spoke the Tejano language. "I was completely ignorant of Spanish, which was indispensable to my success," wrote Abbé Domenech as he struggled to communicate with his Tejano parishioners. And Father Jaillet admitted that "I could not speak twenty words of Spanish."[4]

But the missionaries did not consider the cultural barrier to be their own limitation; rather, they addressed it as a limitation of the Tejanos. The significant conflict, then, was not so much in ritual and canon as it was in the status of Tejanos in the changing government and society of Texas. The greatest barrier that separated Tejanos from priest and Protestant alike was nationality. Ironically, even the French immigrant priests considered the Tejanos to be the foreigners in Texas. As mentioned in the Introduction, newly arrived foreigners in Texas adopted the Anglo-American habit of calling themselves "Texans" after only a few weeks in Texas but referred to Tejanos as "foreigners" or as "Mexicans." This was nowhere more evident than in the written record of the "men of God,"—or in the case of Melinda Rankin, the "woman of God." In one entry to his diary, Father Jaillet wrote that on the Palito Blanco Ranch near San Diego, he and "an American family" encountered a "Mexican," mentioning only incidentally that the "Mexican" was the ranch owner, and that all others were trespassing on his property.

Primarily, the missionaries—both Catholic and Protestant—adhered to the power structure established by the newly arrived Anglo capitalists and considered Tejanos subordinate to the dominant Anglo Americans. Presbyterian missionary Hiram Chamberlain and Catholic Bishop Dominic Manucy of the Corpus Christi diocese courted Richard King, Mifflin Kenedy, and other wealthy Anglos; according to Father Jaillet, they related better and were much closer to the Anglo ranchers than the Tejanos. The Presbyterian Church admitted that their "Anglo prejudice against the Mexicans of Texas made it difficult for potential missionaries to drum up any enthusiasm for their cause."[5] For Tejanos, then, religion remained a communal faith, shared within their own private space on the ranch rather than connecting them to the larger world.

The focal point of religious faith on the Tejano ranch was the chapel altar. There Tejano families prayed, and there the visiting missionaries celebrated religious services. If a ranch had a chapel, the ranch cemetery was located near it and the highest-ranking family members were buried nearest the altar. And even the most modest *jacal* had a little altar or *altarcito,* high in the nook of the bedroom walls. Thus, when Tejanos worshiped, they prayed to their own patron saints, on land that their fathers gave them, and at an altar that they built with their own hands.

The chapel, *la capilla,* was an integral element of the early Tejano ranch long before the missionaries arrived. Across the Tejano ranching frontier, families contributed land and construction materials to build their own chapels. For example, when Don Benito Ramirez built his Rancho Lopeño on the Rio Grande in 1821, he constructed a chapel along with his family house and the fort. On the Trinidad Ranch near San Diego, the Moreno family built their chapel behind the ranch cemetery. The construction of the Trinidad Ranch chapel was marked, reportedly, by the visitation of a wild mustang that stood at the gravesite of Santos Moreno (plate 11). The matriarch of El Randado, Doña Andrea Montalbo, had the Chapel of San Rafael built in 1836, and the ranch's founder, Don Hipolito, was entombed next to it. In typical fashion, the chapel at San Rafael was constructed of *sillar* on a foundation and floor of sandstone *lajas,* and lime was used in the plaster for the walls and the whitewash that was applied inside and out. The chapel had a confessional, pews, an altar with a statue of San Rafael, and a tower with a church bell. According to Randado ranch historian Mary Anna Casstevens, the ladies of the Randado had all contributed jewelry for their chapel bell to be cast in Corpus Christi.

Once the missionaries arrived, they visited chapels all along the Rio Grande, from Laredo to Brownsville. Father Jaillet, for example, held mass in the Tejano chapels at San Diego, Las Peñitas, and Concepción Ranch. The stone schoolhouse at the Buena Vista Ranch, near Laredo, served as the church, ringing its school bell when the priest arrived. The Falcón Ranch further down the river at Zapata had its own permanent chapel for the ranch's one hundred inhabitants, and the Santa María and Toluca Ranches near Edinburg also had their own permanent chapels.

The Methodist mission at El Capote Ranch served a neighboring community of African Americans as well. Before the Civil War, the blacks were slaves who apparently had escaped to something of an underground refuge on El Capote. At the outbreak of the war, the *Brownsville Herald* reported the existence of a sizable Negro colony there, along the Old Military Highway, and announced that the county had officially ordered all "free persons of color" to leave Brownsville within thirty days of the state's secession. The African Americans apparently remained at El Capote, however, and were an integral part of the congregation until after the turn of the century.[6] The old chapel was plowed over for citrus groves that eventually covered the entire ranch, but the tombstones of the little cemetery, surrounded by a solitary grove of oak trees, remained throughout the twentieth century—the only visible sign that there once was a ranch congregation known as El Capote.

Not all ranches had a chapel, of course. Most had only a shrine or a makeshift altar within the courtyard or near the cemetery, beneath a large shade tree. These improvised altars might still be decorated, however, especially when a missionary was to visit; on the San José Ranch, for example, the matrons always came to the patriarch, Don Florencio Guerra, and asked to use his deceased wife's beautifully colored shawls to cover the altar during the mass, and as patriarch, Don Florencio had little choice but agree.[7] On El Tigre Ranch at San Ygnacio, Don Benito Ramirez built a more permanent, carved stone shrine near an *aljibe,* or cistern. Over the well was a carved stone statue of the Virgin of Guadalupe that survived the entire twentieth century. The ranch families on La Encantada had only "two faded religious pictures" at their worship site under a tree; nonetheless the entire family, from the patriarch to the grandchildren and the humblest peons, gathered there every evening to pray the rosary. The space did have a touch of grandeur, for worshipers were shaded by a forty-five-foot-high *sabino,* or Montezuma bald cypress, with a majestic seventy-five-foot crown. This champion *sabino* was approximately eight hundred years old and had a trunk circumference of 225 inches. The families of La Encantada reportedly approached their holy arbor on their knees from "a considerable distance" to hold their daily vespers, or *alabado.*

Vespers was a tradition on many ranches. Each evening, led by the patriarch and matriarch, the entire extended family knelt and prayed:

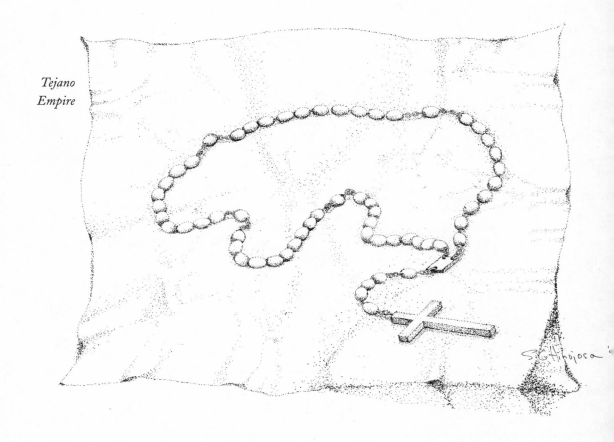

Ave María, madre de Dios,
Llena eres de gracia,
Ruega por nosotros . . .

("Hail, Mary, mother of God,
Thou art full of grace,
Pray for us . . .")

It was particularly ironic that the Tejano patriarchs ritually sponsored—indeed, imposed—vespers for the ranch's extended family, because, according to Jovita González, many of the men had been imbued with liberal and Masonic tendencies when they were educated in Mexico. Tejano men were notorious anti-clerics, perhaps as a way to reciprocate, in their own proud philosophy, against the anti-Mexicanism of the church and the priests. Nonetheless, according to González, they kept all the sacraments, went to church at least three times per year, and attended the nightly vespers.

In her novel, *Caballero,* González captured the patriarch's role in religion.

She described Don Santiago de Mendoza y Soría as he heard the three bells for the evening *alabado:*

The household had orders to wait until the last thread of sound was scattered before the vespers assembly, so the master could have these heart filling moments alone. . . . Servants came out of the rooms opposite, their flat *huaraches* making flapping sounds on the portico floor. Peons came on silent bare feet through the small gate from their quarters outside the wall, dozens of them, from naked infants suckling noisily at bare young breasts down to bent, old people. . . . A few vaqueros from the range camps, burnt almost black by the daily sun and eternal winds, walked stiffly on bowed legs and stood, shy as strangers, just inside the gate, circling worn large hats in nervous fingers. . . . They were all there, everything that supposedly had a soul and therefore had need of prayer . . . and in a rich baritone that filled the patio and drifted over the walls, the master intoned *El Alabado,* the hymn to the Sacrament:

> Alabado sea el Santísimo
> Sacramento del altar
> Y la Virgen concebida
> Sin pecado original.

The chorus, full in its unreserve, surged in harmonious rhythm and Don Santiago, leading and commanding them, felt a kinship with God.[8]

Tejanos prayed aloud, chanting in unison, and often staged formal processions through the courtyard as they chanted. For each feast day, they conducted a special, high ritualized ceremony, such as bathing in the stream and chopping the hair of all Juanas on Saint John's Day, and for such ceremonies they had special chants. Although feast days usually included horse races and dances, the revitalizing spirit of the day was the religious ceremony. On February 2, the Feast of the Virgin of La Candelaria, for example, the priest would come to the ranch to bless the seeds of corn, beans, watermelon, tomato, potato, garbanzo, and squash. On the Feast of Nuestra Señora de los Dolores (or during a drought, as a doleful supplication for rain), Tejanos re-enacted the sorrow (*los dolores*) of Saint Mary as she fell to her knees upon learning of her son's crucifixion. As a healing balm to themselves, they chanted:

> *San Juan, her good nephew, drew nigh,*
> *To lift her fainting form.*
> *'Rise, oh lady, my dear one,*

Rise, loved one of my love,
Lo, on yon bloody Calvary,
Hoarse trumpets are sounding.'

The men led a procession from ranch to ranch, carrying an old, hand-carved wooden statue of Our Lady of Sorrows; the women followed on foot and the children in carts, and the procession gathered additional marchers at each ranch courtyard that it entered. After the religious procession entered the last ranch courtyard, the marchers were invited to a feast and family entertainment, often dancing all night.

Bishop Odin and his priests frequently opposed such traditional Tejano religious rituals as gun salutes and rain prayers, but nonetheless, the priests generally joined the ceremony. They apparently had little choice. Even bishops often found themselves drawn into the elaborate Tejano rituals. In 1866, for example, Bishop Dubuis felt compelled to participate in the procession as he entered San Diego. According to Father Jaillet, "The poor Mexican people took the bows from their wagons, covered them with green branches from the trees and shrubs, and made an arch from the entrance of the town to the door of the little chapel." All the ranch people knelt before the bishop as he passed, and little children "went before him, scattering flowers in his path."[9]

Tejanos typically used elaborate decorations and processions to greet a visiting bishop, especially for major feast days such as Easter or the Feast of the Virgin of Guadalupe. They used blossoms from the shrubs in their gardens and in the chaparral—purple mountain laurel and white guajillo—and wove the green boughs into wreaths, streamers, and draperies. They laced wreaths along the corrals and inner walls of the ranch courtyard and over the main entrance and decorated the altars and the chapel with flowers, lamps, and candles.

The procession began when the chapel bell rang to announce the bishop's arrival at the entry to the archway. There, the patriarch and the men of the ranch greeted the bishop and his retinue, and welcomed them to the ranch. Hundreds of people, dressed in their finest clothes, stood along the archway and the courtyard gate, and as the bishop proceeded through the archway, they knelt and made the sign of the cross. Little girls dressed in white went before him, casting "flowers of the fields and hills" at his feet (although, in one recorded case, a group of little flower girls missed their cue and stood, with their wind-blown hair in their faces and their mouths open in awe at the rare sight of the bishop; they followed behind the bishop, throwing the flowers "after his Grace had passed by, thus making their mothers fret at the disgraceful spectacle they had made.")[10] On processions at the Santa Rita Ranch, the little girls who went before the prelate held a pole ornamented with streamers and flower wreaths, while a young girl behind the flower girls carried an image of the Virgin of Guadalupe.

The crowd, carrying torches and lamps and praying the rosary aloud, then joined the procession behind the bishop and the musicians who played violin, mandolin, and clarinets. As the procession entered the courtyard and gathered at the chapel, they were greeted with a salute of guns and shotguns, and in one case "a rocket." The procession ended as it had begun, with the ringing of the chapel bell.[11] Then the mass was held, and the blessing of *compadres*, babies, and objects took place. Afterward, the families feasted and danced. The priests had the dubious luxury of the chapel as their sleeping quarters, although sleep was difficult until the *tambora de rancho* ceased its loud thumping, usually at dawn. Thus, Tejanos followed their own traditional rituals in welcoming the Roman Catholic clerics.

Guitars, drums, and guns notwithstanding, Tejanos preserved their commitment to the Catholic sacraments. Even the priests who criticized their peculiar rituals admitted that Tejanos on the ranches maintained a devout proficiency in their prayers and knew the basic tenets of the Catholic canon. They prayed the rosary constantly throughout the week, and they diligently taught their children their prayers, memorized by rote rather than through reading. Father Jaillet wrote in his journal in 1866 that though Tejanos were humble, they nevertheless complied with the Catholic church's requirements for religious preparation. He recorded that one ranch couple in San Diego told him, "We are Catholics, though not very good ones." At the same time, he recorded that they had been duly confirmed, like most Tejano adults in the San Diego area. In his first year of arrival in San Diego, he recorded 144 baptisms, 21 marriages, 14 burials, and 79 confirmations.[12] Other priests recognized as well that Tejanos—vaqueros, peons, pastores, patriarchs, and matriarchs—prayed regularly in formal ceremonies with the rest of the ranch family, though they sometimes had to wait several weeks and or even months for a priest to solemnize their wedding vows or perform their child's baptism. For all Tejanos, prayer was an individual experience, but they all joined in formal ceremonies as well.

Mass, of course, was the basic service for Tejano Catholics on the ranch, and it required a visit from a missionary priest. When he arrived, the priest first prepared the altar in the chapel with his sacred vestments, his chalice, and holy water. After the bell had summoned the congregation, he began by singing a few hymns and praying the rosary, with the congregation intoning the Ave Marias in a monotonous unison. He then gave instructions, taught catechism, and ended the evening by hearing confessions. The next morning, he rang the chapel bell for the families from the surrounding ranches to come to mass, and come they did—on horseback, in carts, and on foot, camping out throughout the courtyard as if on a picnic. After communion, the priest quickly exited for the next ranch on his circuit.

Tejanos saw the wedding mass as one of the most solemn and yet festive occasions of ranch life, and they spared no expense or trouble to make it a day of splendor. Often, the bride and groom had already begun living as a married couple, having become espoused through an informal practice called *la tomada de manos*, or "the taking of hands," until the missionary priest could visit the ranch. But the priest's formal validation made the wedding feast all the more joyful for the couple and for the ranch families.

Tejanos referred to the formal wedding ceremony as *la velación*, literally the act of the candle. The groom dressed "all in white" in a linen suit, and the bride dressed in *manta* with lace. In the ceremony, the sponsors or *padrinos* covered the couple jointly with a veil, then held lighted candles as the priest recited the prayers over the bride and groom. In some ceremonies, the groom placed a few coins on a plate for the priest to bless, then handed them over to the bride, almost as if to offer her "the price of her liberty." After the wedding ceremony, everyone celebrated for three or four days, from dusk until dawn, with visiting families camped in the courtyard and the musicians playing all night for the feast and dancing.[13]

Not all religious events were cause for days of dancing, of course. Some, like a childbirth, simply involved a jubilant father firing a pistol into the air to announce the expected birth to the neighboring ranches. Even this was ritualized, however; Tejanos knew that two shots meant it was a girl, and three shots meant it was a boy. The baptism, of course, had to wait until the missionary visit.

Perhaps the most solemn of the religious ceremony was the extreme unction, or the last rites. As Catholics, Tejanos believed that the soul could be cleansed for its acceptance into heaven by a final confession of sins, preferably to a priest, through the formal sacrament of extreme unction. On the remote ranches, Tejanos rarely had the luxury of the formal last rites at their death. When a priest was at hand, it was usually a coincidence. One such case was recorded by Father Jaillet, who happened to be on the trail to Corpus Christi when a young Tejano stopped him and said his mother needed a priest. The priest found the woman lying on a straw mat on the floor of a nearby *jacal*. According to his biography, "Her eyes lit up with joy and hope when she saw the priest." Then she made her last confession and died within fifteen minutes. Actually, Father Jaillet recorded several more such cases, though not so coincidental, during the yellow fever epidemic a few years later. As that scourge raged through the Tejano ranching frontier, he conducted many last rites. In San Diego, for example, "All the way through the town he met wagons carrying the dead out for burial."[14] Thus, whenever Tejano ranches were visited by a priest, the families had a special appreciation for him.

For most Tejanos, death came on the ranch or while they were working or traveling in the chaparral. Tejanos had a tradition of marking a place of death with a cross along the roadside, and travelers through Texas reported roadside crosses as early as 1829, when an official crossed from Mexico City into Texas at Mier on the Rio Grande. After General Zachary Taylor built the Old Military Highway along the north bank of the Rio Grande, another report stated that "Rude crosses, placed along the Camino [road] leading from old Ft. Brown to Ft. Ringgold at its western extension, were a common sight."[15] The Tejano roadside crosses sometimes prompted others to speculate as to whether the deceased was a victim of snakebite, robbery, or hanging, but in any case, they bespoke a message of enduring love and invoked in subsequent travelers a moment of respect, for the deceased if not for the hazardous camino.

When a member of a Tejano family died on the ranch, the ranch families held a funeral mass and a procession to the cemetery. In funeral processions for deceased adults, several men served as pallbearers, and family members and neighbors followed the casket. If they were going to the main ranch house a distance away, the procession stopped at rest stops along the road, and the coffin was placed on a stand called a *descanso,* literally meaning "rest." The mourners also erected roadside crosses with the name of the deceased to mark the places of his *descanso.*

Among Tejanos, the *entierro de un angelito,* or burial of a little angel, was emotionally uplifting. They believed that when an infant died before baptism, its innocent soul went directly to heaven, and the procession took on a distinctive air of "public rejoicing."[16] This, of course, tended to contradict their formal teachings by the Catholic Church regarding unbaptized souls. As a result, one foreign Catholic priest reported that the unorthodox ceremony "put his gravity to a test." The *angelito* was dressed in white with ornamental flowers. In some cases, Abbé Domenech wrote, "wings were added, with a crown of gilt paper." Musicians led the procession, playing waltzes on a violin, a clarinet, and a drum, and an adult, usually the father, carried the tiny casket on his shoulder. Little children followed next, holding candles in their hands. The parents led the rest of the crowd, which was flanked by riflemen who fired gun salutes along the procession. Though the procession seemed to bring relief to the mourners, the French priests along the Tejano ranching frontier, unfortunately, could not see past the gun salutes and the violin.

Few religious events demonstrated the contrast between Tejano beliefs and those of the priests as clearly as the Tejano funeral procession. The Tejano funeral traditions reinforced their group cohesiveness, but the priests rejected the customs that deviated from Catholic canon. Though the priests represented an institution ostensibly there to strengthen the community, the Catholic Church used only foreigners who appeared only to conflict with Tejano beliefs. In their contradictory mission, the Roman Catholic priests were not unlike the Anglo-American teachers who rejected Tejano Spanish. And they were not unlike the Texas Rangers and county sheriffs who were supposed to defend Tejano citizens but who used their weapons to disintegrate the Tejano community.

By the 1880s, as detailed in the epilogue, a number of forces were pushing the Tejano ranch community toward disintegration. As one Tejano ranch after another crumbled and its family moved into Corpus Christi or Anglo-dominated towns like Alice, Raymondville, and McAllen, Tejanos began to turn for spiritual strength to a charismatic faith healer. Around 1883, a Mexican shepherd named Don Pedrito Jaramillo settled on Las Cabras Ranch of Andrés Canales and quickly gained fame as a healer and clairvoyant who cured all manner of diseases for free. Don Pedrito traveled on circuits throughout the ranches, going as far north as San Antonio to heal with prayer and herbal medicines. He returned to his *jacal* on the Olmos Creek to find as many as five hundred believers waiting to be healed. Tejanos may have noticed that most of the five hundred were not Tejanos at all, but instead, newly arrived Mexican immigrants like Don Pedrito himself. But in Don Pedrito, the Tejanos found one person—an institution—who accepted their traditional beliefs. He cured diseases with traditional prayers and chants. He prayed with them. And although priests and medical doctors derided his healing powers, the informal networks of oral communication told Tejanos that he had nevertheless performed near-miracles.[17] They heard, and they believed.

Tejanos had long relied on medicinal herbs and on prayer for healing, and other faith healers had come among them before Don Pedrito. But Don Pedrito was much more than a faith healer. He offered hope that they sorely needed. In their proud ranching tradition, Tejanos had depended on their own patriarchal family networks for their physical and spiritual health. During the 1880s, however, Anglo-American county judges held sheriff's auctions over millions of acres of Tejano family land grants, and commercial farmers from the Midwest plowed over the *casas de sillar* and the patios on ranches from Kingsville to Harlingen. As their ranch world crumbled about them, Tejanos sought to reverse the trend. Unable to turn to the teachers, sheriffs, government officials, or even the priests, they turned to one person who could do as no priest could do—a messianic faith healer who, in his own way, had greater powers than

Richard King and the Texas Rangers. The reality, of course, was that Don Pedrito was powerful only in a spiritual sense and that he could not stop the sheriffs' auctions, the economic trends, or the violence against Tejanos. His messianic appeal served only spiritual needs. His promise led Tejanos nowhere in the temporal world of Anglo-American law and county politics.

A Legacy of Heritage and Conflict

Tejanos founded the ranching frontier on their land grants, and thus were not only leaders of their South Texas communities but also founders of the state of Texas. Without the security of owning their land, they certainly would have developed a different ranching frontier. During the latter nineteenth century, transfer of Tejano titles generally moved in one direction—from Tejano hands into Anglo hands until, most historians agree, after the 1880s Tejanos no longer possessed the bulk of their land grants. Not surprisingly, the loss of their ancestral lands meant the loss of the traditional Tejano ranch culture as well.

Historians have debated the manner in which Tejanos were dispossessed of their lands. Some have argued that most of the lands were stolen, along with the cattle, while others have argued that serious archival research will reveal that most of the lands were transferred legally, though not always ethically. Texas history tells a conflicting story of land transfers from Tejanos to Anglos.

Unfortunately, this period in Texas history was marked by violence, and Tejanos were not its only victims, to be sure. This was, after all, the period of Civil War and Reconstruction. Nevertheless, the story of how Tejanos became dispossessed has been irreversibly tainted by the violence against them on their own lands, from both Anglo bandits and Texas Rangers. This conflict, uniquely combined with their proud Spanish-Mexican heritage, became an essential element in the formation of the modern Tejano identity by the mid-1880s and thus brushed its indelible mark on the character of Texas history. Although late nineteenth-century Tejanos rarely spoke or wrote publicly or officially, much of their history, and much of Texas history, was preserved in the words and deeds of a few articulate Tejanos.

Over the years, 2,261 Tejanos registered land grants with the Texas General Land Office in Austin. Some of them took their titles from the King of Spain, and others from the Republic of Mexico, through the municipalities of the Villas del Norte. Still others took grants as headrights under the Republic of Texas, and many of them claimed Bounty, Donation, and pre-emption grants under the State of Texas. All of these Tejanos received their land grants for service on the frontier. Unfortunately, for one reason or another, most Tejano grantees never patented or confirmed their titles. The result was that in the San Antonio and Victoria areas, three-fourths of the Tejano grantees lost their patents, and south of the Nueces, about one-third of them lost their patents. And many who did patent their titles later lost their lands through other means.

The government of Texas played a role in weakening the Tejanos' hold on their land titles. The Bourland and Miller Commission of 1852, as mentioned earlier, lost many of the original titles in the sinking of the steamship *Anson,* although the state confirmed most of the rest of the titles it reviewed. Subsequent Texas laws and court cases continued to threaten the validity of Tejano land grants. The Relinquishment Law of 1852, for example, required that all Tejano land titles be filed with the General Land Office in Austin, or they would be declared null and void. This law became part of the Texas Constitution of 1876, although it was eventually declared unconstitutional by *Gonzales v. Ross* in 1886.

The case of Lazaro Garza illustrates the plight of many Tejanos who struggled over the years to retain title to their land. In accordance with the Relinquishment Law, Garza had to take his claim to the capital in Austin, where in 1857 he declared to the Texas Legislature that he was the equal of any Anglo American, and demanded his land. Garza's case demonstrates what Tejanos had to struggle against—racial prejudice from the very legislators who were supposed to represent their interests at the state level. Garza, an older gentleman, had been told that a committee rule required that in order for Tejanos to testify as U.S. citizens of Mexican origin, "their character for truth and veracity had to be established by the testimony of two white men." Garza declared to the legislative committee that "before he would submit to the indignity . . . he would willingly lose every cent of money and every inch of land to which he might justly be entitled."[1]

The legal struggle, unfortunately, was even more intense at the local level, where the old Tejano ranch owners had to contend with men like Hidalgo County Judge Thaddeus Rhodes and Starr County Judge N. P. Norton. Tejanos lost much of their land to Anglo capitalists and adventurers who took advantage of the new county courts and outright violence to harass Tejanos and drive them into hiding, then used sheriff's auctions to claim their lands during the Tejanos' absence. Famous rancher Richard King, Hidalgo County Judge Rhodes, and other so-called *"robavacas,"* or "cattle rustlers," financed cattle rustling operations in Hidalgo County ranches. King's rustlers were led by a man named Tomás Vasquez, according to an Investigative Committee Report *(Informe de la Comisión Pesquisidora)* published in Mexico in 1874. King also kept a band of hired guns on his ranch, whom the Tejano ranchers called *"los rinches de la kineña,"* meaning "the Rangers of the King Ranch," to insulate him personally from his rustling operation. Indeed, a modern King Ranch archivist admitted that King "utilized armed force, not always legally deputized."[2] Meanwhile, his lawyers perfected their legal claims to the Tejano lands to preclude future litigation.

In Hidalgo County, Judge Rhodes reportedly supported a gang of thirty cattle rustlers on his Rosario Ranch. They regularly raided local ranches and traded in stolen livestock. According to Hidalgo County Court Records and the Mexican Investigative Committee, Rhodes was imprisoned in 1858 when stolen cattle were found on his ranch, but he was released and later returned to impose sheriff's auctions against many parcels of land belonging to Tejano ranchers.[3]

In Starr County, Tejano ranchers had to protect their lands and cattle from Anglo lawmen as well as Anglo bandits, and in too many cases, the lawmen and bandits were one and the same. For example, Starr County District Judge N. P. Norton personally led his *robavacas* on cattle rustling raids against Tejano ranches. On March 26, 1853, he led a gang of fifty bandits who sacked Reynosa, in Mexico, and held Alcalde Trinidad Flores hostage for a ransom of 30,000 pesos. Judge Norton took the town's cattle and livestock and escaped by crossing the Rio Grande into Texas. Court records indicate that charges for this incident were filed against Norton in Brownsville, but he avoided conviction because of his privileged position. He then returned to continue his rustling operation. To protect their own land and business interests from avaricious Anglo Americans and from Mexican rustlers who crossed the Rio Grande to steal Tejano cattle as well, many Tejano ranchers such as Santos Benavides and Santiago Vidaurri eventually had to lead small mounted bands along the river and fight off attacks on all sides.[4] The Tejanos managed to defend themselves against minor attacks from Mexico, but they eventually lost ground to the large-scale vigilante sweeps emanating from the King Ranch and to the Texas Rangers who systematically targeted Tejanos.

One of the most devastating vigilante raids, and revealing of King's background role, was the Peñascal Raid of 1874, also known as the Second Cortina War and the Skinning War. A vigilante committee of about one hundred Anglos and at least some "Mexicans" from Corpus Christi set out ostensibly to avenge the murder of four Anglos by "Mexicans" at a store near Corpus Christi. One of the "Mexicans" who plotted and led the murder at the store was later identified by Ranger J. B. Dunn as "Tom Bosquez" of Corpus Christi—evidently Richard King's henchman, Tomás Vásquez.[5] For several months prior to the raids, King and others had complained about the Tejano ranches, including the Atravesada, La Parra, El Corral de Piedra, and El Mesquite, as well as the Peñascal Ranch in present-day Kenedy County, about sixty miles south of Corpus Christi. These ranches were home to about five hundred Tejano men, women, and children.

King and others accused vaqueros from the Tejano ranches of stealing cattle, but it was the murder of the Anglos at the store that sparked the raid. A vigilante posse from Corpus Christi gathered at King's ranch for his guidance. King instructed them to elect leaders—about twenty men—who should go first to Brownsville to be deputized. After being deputized, the posse returned to King "to receive instructions." If there were killings, they asked, "would King stand by the deputies?" He replied "that he would see them justified." With their instructions, and acting under color of law, the deputies then masked and painted themselves, took up arms, and set out at around midnight, "full of mescal and drunk."[6] They threw coal oil on the thatched roofs of the houses and stores at the ranches and systematically killed all of the Tejano patriarchs and "every adult male that was present."[7]

They swept through all of the nearby Tejano ranches. Encarnación Morales and his brother Guadalupe were the first to be attacked, at the ranch store where they worked on La Atravesada Ranch. In the presence of the Morales family, ten Anglos surrounded the store and shot Guadalupe to death as he went to open the door. Encarnación and the rest of the family escaped as the raiders burned the store. As the raiders swept through one ranch after another, the women and children fled into the chaparral and hid throughout the night. At daylight, only the chimneys of the ranch houses remained standing amid smoldering ashes. Many of the men's bodies were never found and were presumed to have been "dumped in the bay." On April 18, 1875, the Corpus Christi sheriff wired a telegram to Austin. His message read: "IS CAPT [Ranger L. H.] MCNELLY COMING. WE ARE IN TROUBLE. FIVE RANCHES BURNED BY DISGUISED MEN NEAR LAPARRA LAST WEEK. ANSWER." McNelly arrived and wrote back to Austin: "The acts committed by Americans are horrible to relate; many ranches have been plundered and burned, and the people murdered or driven away; one of these parties confessed to me in Corpus Christi as having killed eleven men on their last raid."[8]

After the Peñascal Raid, most of the lands involved were incorporated into the King and Kenedy ranch empires, as the women and children and other Tejano rancheros fled across the border to the Villas del Norte. According to one account: "They departed taking their money and personal possessions with them, and often they were found dead along the way with their money missing." Eulalia Tijerina, whose store was destroyed, was one of the few who remained, though her land was subsequently incorporated into the Kenedy Ranch. According to Faustino Morales of Kenedy County, Mifflin Kenedy "didn't have water in his pasture and Mrs. Tijerina had a big lake in hers. He fenced in all of the lake to his property. . . . That's what he always fought for—water—he didn't have any." The surviving vaqueros eventually went to work for Kenedy, King, and the other Anglo ranchers who took possession of their lands.[9] King's hired gun, Tomás Vásquez, who evidently was present when the four Anglos were murdered at the store, became a member of the police force in Corpus Christi.

While vigilante raids were vicious, they probably were not as devastating in undermining the Tejano ranching frontier as the murders by Texas Rangers. The Rangers were acting under the auspices of the government of Texas, in collaboration with Anglo ranchers, and to the applause of many historians and the public. When the agents of the state began summarily to kill Tejano ranchers with gusto, the government's credibility with Tejanos was seriously compromised. On May 17, 1885, for example, the Laredo ranch community was shocked when a Tejano patriarch was shot and killed in an ambush by Texas Ranger B. D. Lindsay and other rangers, in what the Tejanos could only interpret as an example of cowardice and deception. When Lindsay and his fellow Rangers saw the elder gentleman, a "well-known citizen of good repute," riding alongside two younger men, they gave no notice but shot first at the older gentleman. The younger Tejanos returned fire, killing and wounding some of their attackers. But the image became fixed in the Tejano ranch frontier that the Texas Rangers were targeting the patriarchs for assassination.[10]

Although many Anglos had an image of the Rangers as brave and straightforward, the Abbé Domenech, a disinterested visitor, observed: "The greater part of the murders were committed by the Rangers—volunteers of the American army who were disbanded after the treaty of Guadalupe Hidalgo, and had engaged themselves to Texas for the pursuit of the Indians. They are the very dregs of society, and the most degraded of human creatures." Some of the most critical descriptions came from the Rangers themselves. J. B. "Red" Dunn

wrote in his memoirs that he and other unemployed men were recruited into a Texas Ranger unit formed in the Corpus Christi area and containing "the worst mixed lot of men that ever came together in one organization. . . [and] some of the most dilapidated, diseased, moth-eaten specimens of humanity that I have ever seen. Some of them could not stay on a trotting horse." Dunn said that he and his brother had been "given to understand that if certain ones of us would return to Santa Gertrudis [the King Ranch] and go into camp there, we would be sent commissions in a few weeks and be put on the State Police Force that was being organized at that time" to replace the traditional Ranger frontier patrols. The Dunn brothers "worked for Captain King for three months."[11]

The Rangers drew similar criticism from contemporary Texas newspapers and from legislators as well. They were most distrusted for their methods and their use of *ley fuga,* the Ranger practice of shooting handcuffed prisoners in the back without benefit of trial. By the 1880s, Tejanos had developed a definite image of the Texas Rangers as singling out Tejano political and family leaders for assassination, with the "crowding out" of the Mexican ranchers.[12]

One by one, the Tejano families abandoned their ranches and fled to Mexico rather than lose a loved one to the campaign of violence. The *casas de sillar* fell into disrepair, taxes fell into arrears, and Anglo speculators purchased the lands at sheriff's auctions.

The Hidalgo County sheriff's auction of the old El Capote Ranch typified the shoddy transfer of land from Tejanos to Anglos. When the old Spanish *porción* land grant of Juan José Hinojosa went into tax arrears in 1877, a 3,027-acre Tejano ranch on the land grant sold at the sheriff's auction for a total cash price of fifteen dollars. The following year, the remaining 4,000 acres of fertile delta soil sold for $17.75. Within five years, Anglo commercial farmers began to till the soil. The Anglo farmers later claimed that the Mexicans simply had no appreciation of the land, but this hardly seems compatible with the Tejanos' long history on their family lands.[13] While there may have been some Tejano landowners who squandered their patrimony, many Tejano families tell quite a different story about how they lost their lands.

According to Doña Josefa Guerra de Benavides, Don Pedro Guerra and his family owned a ranch on the road to San Antonio. He caught three Mexican cattle rustlers on his land and killed one of them in the ensuing gunfight. Don Pedro volunteered himself to the County Court, where he was acquitted for self-defense in a trial at Cotulla. The incident brought him some fame as a paragon of Tejano pride, and he began to hear rumors that the Texas Rangers had targeted him for assassination. As Mrs. Guerra related the story, two Texas Rangers came into the ranch one day, asking for Don Pedro and laughing "that they had never seen a Mexican brave enough to stand up for his rights and would like to set eyes on one." Don Pedro and his family quickly concluded that the Rangers had no admiration or good will for such a Tejano, and the Guerras fled to Mexico, abandoning their land grant, ranch, and *casa de sillar.* As Doña Josepha concluded: "crumbling walls now attest to the terror of the *'rinches'* that lived in the hearts of even honest men."[14]

While the Tejano victims and their families told stories of ambush and brutality, the Texas Rangers usually recorded events quite differently, telling of tall men with intrepid hearts, arresting Mexican bandits who deserved to die. Unfortunately, the truth usually died with the victims, there being no modern videotapes whirring from behind the bushes to capture the action. But in one rare incident, there was a Tejano—a very quiet Tejano—watching from a windmill, and the story that he told was the mirror image of the story recorded by the Texas Rangers and by their historian par excellence, Walter Prescott Webb.

According to Webb's published account in *The Texas Rangers,* on a ranch adjacent to the King Ranch, "Rangers found two or three unbranded calves tied to bushes or trees, and feeling sure that their game was near, they scattered to search the brush. Sergeant Baker soon came upon a Mexican who was in the act of branding a calf. The Mexican, armed with two six-shooters, fired at Baker . . . Baker shot the Mexican in the head with a soft-nosed Winchester bullet. The dead man was recognized as Ramon De La Cerda whose family owned a small ranch adjoining the King estate." The Rangers later tracked the man's father, Ramon de la Cerda, Sr., to Brownsville, where they also killed him.[15]

The Tejano version was recorded by Roberto Villareal, a descendant of a Tejano ranching family whose lands came to belong to the King and Kenedy ranches. Villareal personally interviewed Simon Villareal, whose mother was a servant at the de la Cerda family ranch at the time of the incident and had provided a first-hand account. According to Villareal, Jesse Miller, a King Ranch employee, invited Ramon de la Cerda to a fiesta on the King Ranch, but when de la Cerda "got to the appointed place[,] instead of a fiesta he rode into an ambush. The three Texas Rangers who murdered Ramon de la Cerda, Jr., including one named 'Bekar' [Baker], had also arranged to have some calves at the scene to use as evidence. However, a King Ranch worker, who had been working on a nearby windmill, and who had not been noticed by the Rangers, witnessed the incident and reported it to the family." Villareal's account added that the Rangers had to ambush de la Cerda because he had a reputation for bravery and his father for skill with a rifle. According to Villareal, the Rangers did not kill de la Cerda's father in Brownsville, as Webb wrote, but his brother, Alfredo de la Cerda, whom they shot through the window of a store while he was trying on some gloves. They then killed the patriarch, Ramon de la Cerda, Sr., in an ambush on his ranch, prompting the family's youngest son to abandon the ranch and flee to Mexico.

While the King Ranch continued to acquire Tejano ranches, the Kenedy Ranch was also expanding. It acquired ten surrounding Tejano ranches, averaging about 25,000 acres each, including Las Motas de Barreta of Don Leonardo Salinas, El Palmito of Don Miguel Ynojosa, Los Finados of Don Juan N. de la Garza, La Parra of Don Alvino de la Garza, El Paistle of Don Juan Antonio Ballí, El Rincon de Peñascal, Rincon de Mirasoles of Don Ignacio Villareal, Los Tajos of Don Juan Antonio Ballí, San Pedro de las Motas of Don Xavier Salinas, and Las Barrosas of Don Irineo Gomez. The Anglo capitalist ranchers used their lawyers to perfect the land titles and preclude future lawsuits that might question their acquisition of these lands. They then justified their acquisition of Tejano lands because, notwithstanding the violence and sheriff's auctions, it was "legal." Unlike the Tejano ranchers, Anglo business men did not have to have ready cash because they could obtain bank loans in San Antonio. Thus in many cases, their acquisitions were legitimate purchases from financially pressed Tejana widows or Tejano pensioners who sold out to a businessman. In her study of the Victoria area, Ana Caroline Castillo Crimm found a variety of factors for the land dispossession. As in the Kingsville area, her study found Anglo squatters and sheriff auction buyers swearing "to defend their land even if they had to use violence to remove the Mexicans who were trying to reclaim their land through law suits." She added, however, "The greatest land loss came when inherited lands were sold after having been divided into sections too small to ranch." In her final analysis, Crimm concluded that as much was lost to Anglos as was retained by Tejanos. She cited the case of Fernando de León who lost 50,000 acres to sheriffs' auctions after he was driven out of Victoria after the Texas Revolution, but who returned after 1846 to successfully defend another 50,000 acres through litigation. She considered de León's case as a poor example of "racist oppression." As David Montejano explained in his study of King Ranch acquisitions, the man with exclusive access to Anglo banks had only to wait until the drought forced Tejanos to sell.[16]

The Tejanos were thus dispossessed of their lands, with devastating effects on the Tejano ranch community. As Tejanos lost their lands, they became farmworkers, or they moved into the South Texas towns that were controlled by the very political and economic forces that had forced the land transfer. Robert Kleberg, the King Ranch lawyer, and politician Jim Wells controlled county politics. Indeed, the very names of Kleberg and Jim Wells Counties indicated their power. Fermina Guerra aptly described this transition in the Laredo area: "the 'Gringos,' came with their suspicions and impatience with the easy going Mexican 'vaquero.' These newcomers crowded out the small ranchman by force of greater financial resources, by their knowledge of loopholes in the law, often by force alone." As the Tejano families sold or abandoned their ranches, she wrote, "The vaquero became the cotton picker and the day laborer."[17]

Many Tejanos managed to survive the land dispossession, as indicated by Castillo Crimm. Another study of Hidalgo County revealed that many Tejanos successfully transitioned to a capitalist ranching structure or to businesses in town. Armando Alonzo stated in this study, "Still, Tejanos played a leading role in the commercialization of ranching and participated in other economic activities, assisting in the growth of the national economy; they held onto their lands and utilized them as best they could to the very end of the century, forging a distinctive identity and heritage that newcomers could not dissolve." Both Alonzo and Crimm cited numerous examples, along with Mary Anna Casstevens's study of the Randado, in which Tejanos were anything but hopeless victims. Although all three of these studies found ample cases of Anglo racism and violence against Tejanos, their documented findings give reason enough to believe that Tejanos urbanized and transitioned in response to other factors as well. By the end of the 1880s, many Tejano ranch families were nevertheless working as migrant farm workers on the very lands that their fathers had owned only a few years earlier. The Garza family of El Capote Ranch was typical of this transition. The family had, of course, operated El Capote Ranch on their grant of Juan José Hinojosa, from the Villa del Norte of Reynosa. In the end, their land was transferred to Sheriff John Closner and his partner, Jim Wells. Closner grew wealthy on commercial farming in "The Magic Valley" as an investor of the Louisiana-Rio Grande Canal Company. Meanwhile, Roberto and Nestor Garza, scions of El Capote Ranch, became labor contractors for migrant workers in the cotton fields and citrus packing sheds in Edinburg.[18]

As members of the Tejano ranch families moved to cities or became part of the migrant labor circuit, many of their ranches became Anglo ranches or corporate citrus farms. Their cattle were driven north to Kansas. The story of the Tejano ranching frontier became little more than a parenthetical backdrop in the history of the Anglo-American frontier and the Anglo-American cowboy. The colorful history that Walter Prescott Webb told in his award-winning book, *The Great Plains,* describes the "Cattle Kingdom," the great cattle kings, and the famous cattle trails as exclusively Anglo-American phenomena. In Webb's history, the cattle trails began and ended in Anglo-American cities, rather than in Tejano towns and ranches where the cattle were produced. Ironically, because dispossessed Tejano grandchildren learned American history in the towns they moved into, they never learned the names of the Tejano towns and ranches at the southern end of the historic cattle trails. The story of the old Tejano ranches became lost beneath the famous stories of wealthy Anglo-American ranching corporations, and ranches like El Randado, Los Ojuelos, and La Parra became living ghosts. Their disappearance from the history taught to Tejano schoolchildren was the culmination of Anglo domination in South Texas.

A graphic example of Webb's history was seen in his famous book, *The Great Plains,* in which he described the Texas Cattle Kingdom. Webb described the Cattle Kingdom as five million cattle in a diamond-shaped region between San Antonio, Laredo, Brownsville, and the Gulf Coast. He wrote "On the northeast side of the diamond, then stood the future [Anglo] cowboys; on the southwest line were the Mexican cattle." Webb simply omitted the 10,000 Tejanos living on the hundreds of ranches that produced the millions of cows. Another author, Terry G. Jordan, presented a largely race-based argument that there were insignificant numbers of Tejanos in South Texas.

Jordan simply dismissed Tejano ranchers, arguing that Texas ranching was actually an Anglo-American industry from the Atlantic Coast. Indeed, Armando Alonzo has argued in his demographic study of ranching that by 1880, there was a population of 51,826 in the South Texas ranching towns and counties, 85 percent of whom were Tejano.[19] Nevertheless, Jordan's simplistic omission carried into the history of Texas that was taught for the remainder of the twentieth century to Anglo and Tejano children alike. The domination of Tejano lands and Tejano families that began when the Texas Rangers, judges, sheriffs, and posses swept through the ranches, reached its final phase when Tejano grandchildren in Kingsville, San Diego, and Corpus Christi learned to recite Jordan's and Webb's version of ranching history.

In the process of domination, however, resistance—like hope—springs eternal in the human breast. Indeed, the Tejano story was not one of simple domination but rather, as described by historian James C. Scott, "domination and the art of resistance." At home, Tejanos continued to teach their children the same values and culture that they had learned from their own parents on the ranches. And though they were pressured to forsake their Mexican heritage and acculturate to the Anglo culture, they kept alive their folklore, their music, and their beliefs. Though Tejano Spanish was considered only an illegitimate pidgin language, they retained it at home, hidden from their Anglo teachers who taught only European Spanish. In the privacy of their own space, Tejanos preserved the values that their descendants would search for a hundred years later among the archives and records of a research library.

The struggle of resistance was as challenging and as brutal for Tejanos in early twentieth-century Texas as the struggle of their grandparents had been. Indeed, the Tejano ranching frontier would have died a quiet death if it had not been for a precious few Tejano historians who preserved it in their writings in family histories or in master's theses. Their faint voices in a wilderness of history managed to preserve the Tejano ranch story. And these historians took their cue from an even more precious few Tejano leaders who, even as the Tejano rancheros were being driven from their lands, issued the last defiant declarations of the Tejano ranching frontier. Four of these defiant Tejanos were Juan Nepomuceno Cortina, José Antonio Navarro, Angel Navarro, and J. T. Canales.

Cortina, the Navarros, and Canales were all imbued with the heritage of the original Tejano community of Texas. All distinguished themselves not only as leaders, but as men who could no longer tolerate silence. Each of them unleashed a verbal outburst that resounded throughout Texas, from the chaparral to the state legislature in Austin. In this way, they broke the silence that the Abbé Domenech saw in Tejanos in 1860 when he wrote: "the Mexican might have an easy vengeance on his persecutors, who are quite the minority on the Texian frontiers, but vengeance is not in his heart." The defiant Tejanos sought not vengeance, but justice and legitimacy.

In 1859, Cortina led hundreds of Tejanos in the Brownsville area in a futile effort to strike back at the economic, military, and political forces that took Tejano lands and dignity. Although Texas history has condemned him as an illiterate "Mexican bandit," Cortina posted circulars invoking the same social contract as Thomas Jefferson in his declaration of American independence: "To defend ourselves, and making use of the sacred right of self-preservation, we have assembled in a popular meeting." Cortina identified the individuals who had conspired against Tejano ranchers and enumerated his grievances. Naming the land lawyers, he said: "These . . . form, with a multitude of lawyers, a secret conclave, with all its ramifications, for the sole purpose of despoiling the Mexicans of their lands and usurp them afterwards. This is clearly proven by the conduct of one Alolph Glavecke, who, invested with the character of deputy sheriff, and in collusion with the said lawyers, has spread terror among the unwary, making them believe that he will hang the Mexicans and burn their ranches, &c., that by this means he might compel them to abandon the country, and thus accomplish their object . . . and even more, are capable such criminal men as the one last mentioned, the marshal, the jailer, Morris, Neal, &c." When the U.S. Army overpowered Cortina, he was forced to flee to Mexico and resorted to violence, swearing: "Further, our personal enemies shall not possess our lands until they have fattened it with their own gore."[20]

Angel Navarro of San Antonio defended the rights of Tejano land claimants in Austin. As a state legislator, Navarro personally stood against the entire Anglo legislature in 1857 to defend Lazaro Garza, the Tejano land claimant who argued for his rights before the legislature. In defense of Garza, Navarro said he was not asking for pity but for equal protection under the law for "citizens of Mexican origin." In a subtle declaration of Tejano pride, he added: "If this race of people, Mr. Speaker, be inferior to the actual governing race in this country, and if in the natural course of things, it must disappear and be supplanted by the superior Anglo-Saxon race, let us not permit that this be done by means of our legislation."[21]

Angel's father, José Antonio Navarro, likewise spoke for all Tejanos in 1855. The elder Navarro, who had served in the Texas Revolution, resented the implication that only Anglo-Americans had fought and died for Texas independence—and that Tejanos were not legitimately entitled to the fruits of liberty in Texas. He declared that Tejanos were the only "legitimate" heroes of Texas Independence; the Anglos were only newcomers to the struggle for Texas independence, while Tejanos had liberated Texas from hostile American Indians as well as from the Spaniards. Tejanos had even fought against Mexico for the Republic of Texas. But because they were considered "Mexicans," they were being driven from their native land. Navarro was particularly resentful that the Alamo was called "the shrine" of Texas independence in 1836, in complete disregard for the thousands of Tejanos who had died for Texas' freedom from Spain in 1821. Defending the Tejano patriots, Navarro said, "To complete the picture of their misfortunes, their few descendants yet surviving in San Antonio, are disappearing, the victims of assassination, in sight of a people which claims the blazon of justice and grandeur as theirs 'par excellence.'" He called Tejanos "this race of men who, legitimate lords of this country, lost it with their lives and their hopes in following on the traces of the very people who now enjoy it in the midst of peace and abundance."[22]

Another defiant Tejano at the end of the nineteenth century was J. T. Canales of Las Cabras Ranch near Falfurrias, who became a judge, state legislator, and advocate of Tejano rights, specifically against the Texas Rangers. At the risk of his own life—and in a near fistfight on the floor of the House chambers—Canales boldly articulated the grievances and demands of the Tejano community. He succeeded in forcing a review of the Rangers' conduct, charging them with "wanton killing, flogging and torture of prisoners, drunkenness, and assault." His bill in the legislature led eventually to the Ranger force being reduced and reorganized, albeit slightly.

The Rangers and their supporters in South Texas and in the legislature assumed an aggressive posture against Canales. One Ranger even threatened him on the steps of the capitol in Austin, so it surprised no one when he announced: "my life is threatened by a Ranger now in the service of the State of Texas." During the hearings, William G. B. Morrison, a South Texan, implied that the Rangers, who had been accused of "killing from five hundred to five thousand men," had been justified, and that "the citizens killed as many as the Rangers." Throughout the hearings, however, legislators and news accounts admitted that Canales objectively addressed the problem. Indeed, in his objectivity, Canales articulated the Tejano position for the Tejano community when he declared "that we believe the Texas Ranger force is an element of safety in the enforcement of laws if such force can be kept free from politics as the original force was; but it is a dangerous element and a menace to the citizens if the Ranger force is used for political purposes." Canales drew a violent response, even in the House chambers.

When he accused Lubbock representative W. H. Bledsoe of misrepresenting his statement, Bledsoe walked across the aisle and leaned over Canales's desk, shaking his fist in the Tejano's face and saying, "Mr. Canales, if you dare again to open your mouth to intimate that anything I may say is an untruth, I will slap you on the jaw if it costs me my seat in the House." Canales stood and challenged him: "Go ahead and slap it." The two men stood staring into each other's eyes for a full minute, according to a newspaper reporter, "while the Speaker rapped like a trip hammer with his gavel, and the sergeant at arms advanced down the aisle to interpose, and members stood and half rose from their seats the better to see what would happen." But Canales held his position and pressed Tejano rights until one entire unit of the Rangers was disbanded and the force slightly reduced.[23]

Public outbursts of this type by Tejanos were rare, but they revealed much. In these outbursts, Tejanos gave vent to the secret feelings of their community. Their declarations were valuable because they could be assumed to be true. When one of these Tejanos unleashed a public outburst against Anglo domination, he did it "in the teeth of power," and he did it with the sure knowledge that there would be retaliation. But his defiant stand made it clear to his opponents that he was prepared to accept the consequences. It was truth manifest, for even his opponents knew that he had no reason to lie under those circumstances. In such public declarations, the Tejano advocated for his community, not just for himself.[24] He spoke not of his own personal financial losses, but for the right of self-preservation, for Tejano legitimacy, and against abuses directed toward his people because of race. Texas history books have tended to ignore or to minimize these Tejano declarations, but the statements were significant because they were the words of the contemporary Tejanos, articulating the otherwise hidden feelings of the men, women, and children of the Tejano ranching frontier.

One other group of defiant Tejanos has emerged in the twentieth century to rectify the plight of their ancestors. Tejano land claimants began to organize legal claims against the some of the large landowners who had taken over the Tejano lands, such as the King Ranch, the Kenedy Ranch, and the O'Connor Ranch. The Becerra Family Association is typical: modern Tejano descendants have organized to regain, through litigation, the lost lands of the Ballí, de la Garza, and Becerra families, among others. The leaders of the modern ranching corporations typically respond that their corporate lawyers have long since perfected their legal titles, but they seem to understand that they will not soon see the end of the Tejano land claimants, such as historian and land claimant Abel G. Rubio of "the poor but proud Becerra family." Rubio, whose family sued the O'Connor ranching corporation, wrote a book about his family's continuing dream to "share the fruits of Don Manuel Becerra's stolen heritage."[25] Rubio's comments left no doubt that Tejanos would never resign themselves to seeing others enjoy wealth on Tejano lands taken through violence. The loss of Tejano lands is not only a dynamic issue, but one that strikes at the heart of Tejano identity.

Whether Tejano descendants will ever regain their ancestral lands has become a continuing question in Texas history. Thus far, their only recourse has been through the courts and has proven to be a costly and lengthy process. Indeed, the 1850 Texas Land Commissioner James B. Miller predicted they would be better served by other methods than trying to "sue it out through the courts." When the Anglos wanted Tejano lands, they had a state legislative commission to help them release the Tejanos' control. Neither the dispossessed Tejanos nor their descendants have ever had the luxury of a Tejano Land Commission to review the violence or the illegality behind transferred titles. This ironic fact, of course, has also been a part of the tainted history of Texas lands. The lost Tejano lands represent the unique combination of the Tejano identity as well as Texas history. It is a story of rich heritage and dynamic conflict.

Tejano ranch life of the nineteenth century provided not only the daily needs of the families, but more importantly, it provided a repository of Tejano culture. In many ways, Tejanos were hidden on the ranches. There they were the masters of their own family life, their work, and their land. They preserved their traditional culture, orally for the most part, through their ranch schools and their family legends. Their community rituals, family values, and religious beliefs formed the sense of community that Tejanos struggled to preserve during the radical transition period at the end of the nineteenth century. Their history in the ranch communities gave them a point of reference as they and their children became urbanized in the early twentieth century. Their early ranch experience also gave their political leaders a strong sense of the social and political issues they would need to defend in such later organizations as LULAC and the American G.I. Forum. Certainly the twentieth-century Hispanic community was different from the nineteenth-century *rancho* community, but the values that modern Hispanics so often articulated, the culture they sang about in their music, and the issues that their community leaders came to defend had their origins on the nineteenth-century Tejano ranching frontier.

Introduction

1. The *frontera* concept is discussed in Andrés Tijerina, *Tejanos and Texas under the Mexican Flag, 1821–1836* (College Station: Texas A&M University Press, 1994); Alicia Hinojosa, *The Hinojosa Family: From Mier, Tamaulipas, Mexico to Texas* (Utica, Kans.: McDowell Publications, 1992), p. 10.

2. David Martel Vigness, "The Republic of the Rio Grande: An Example of Separatism in Northern Mexico" (Ph.D. diss., University of Texas, 1951), pp. 148, 149.

3. K. Jack Bauer, *The Mexican War, 1846–1848* (Lincoln: University of Nebraska Press, 1974), p. 36; José María Roa Barcena, *Recuerdos de la invasion norteamericana (1846–1848),* Tomo I (Mexico: Editorial Porrua, 1947), pp. 61–65.

4. Mirabeau B. Lamar, *Papers of Mirabeau Buonaparte Lamar,* 6 vols. (Austin: A. C. Baldwin and Sons, [1921–27]): vol. 4, part 1, p. 196.

5. Américo Paredes, *With His Pistol in His Hand: A Border Ballad and Its Hero* (Austin: University of Texas Press, 1958), p. 15.

6. Brian Robertson, *Wild Horse Desert: The Heritage of South Texas* (Edinburg: New Santander Press, 1985), pp. 89, 90.

7. David Montejano, *Anglos and Mexicans in the Making of Texas, 1836–1886* (Austin: University of Texas Press, 1987), p. 72.

8. *Informe de La Comisión Pesquisidora de la Frontera del Norte al Ejecutivo de la Union* (Monterrey: Imprenta de Diaz de Leon y White, 1874), p. 68; Valley By-Liners, *Rio Grande Roundup: Story of Texas Tropical Borderlands* (Mission: Border Kingdom Press, 1980), p. 61.

9. Roberto M. Villareal, "The Mexican-American Vaqueros of the Kenedy Ranch: A Social History" (Master's thesis, Texas A&I University, 1972), p. 2.

10. Galen D. Greaser and Jesús de la Teja, "Quieting Title to Spanish and Mexican Land Grants in the Trans-Nueces: The Bourland and Miller Commission, 1850–1852," *Southwestern Historical Quarterly* 95, no. 4 (Apr., 1992): 455, 457n; Texas General Land Office, "Report of James R. Miller & W.H. Bourland, Commissioners to Investigate Land Titles West of the Nueces, (*MSS* 1854, Spanish Collection, Archives and Records Division); Robertson, *Wild Horse Desert,* pp. 76, 77.

11. Armando C. Alonzo, "Change and Continuity in Tejano Ranches in the Trans-Nueces, 1848–1900" in Joe S. Graham, ed., *Proceedings of "Ranching in South Texas: A Symposium"* (Kingsville: Texas A&M University, Kingsville, 1994), p. 62.

Chapter 1. Las Villas del Norte

1. Jack Jackson, *Los Mesteños: Spanish Ranching in Texas, 1721–1821* (College Station: Texas A&M University Press, 1986); Virgil N. Lott and Mercurio Martinez, *The Kingdom of Zapata* (San Antonio: The Naylor Company, 1953), p. 60.

2. Abbé Domenech, *Missionary Adventures in Texas and Mexico: A Personal Narrative of Six Years' Sojourn in Those Regions* (London: Longman, Brown, Green, Longmans, and Roberts, 1858), p. 64. For a fuller description of *sacate de bestia*, see Fermina Guerra, "Mexican and Spanish Folklore and Incidents in Southwest Texas" (Master's thesis, University of Texas, 1941), p. 40.

3. Ibid., p. 87.

4. Margaret McAllen, *The Heritage Sampler: Selections from the Rich and Colorful History of the Rio Grande Valley* (Edinburg: New Santander Press, 1991), p. 77.

5. Eugene George, *The Historic Architecture of Texas: The Falcón Reservoir* (Austin: Texas Historical Commission, 1975), p. 53; Lott and Martinez, *Kingdom of Zapata*, p. 7; Zapata County, "Zapata Folklore" (unpublished booklet in Zapata County Museum, n.d.), p. 10.

6. George, *Historic Architecture*, p. 53; Lott and Martinez, *Kingdom of Zapata*, p. 89; Jean Y. Fish, *José Vasquez Borrego and La Hacienda de Nuestra Señora de Dolores* (Zapata, Tex.: Zapata County Historical Society, 1991), p. 17.

7. F. Michael Black, comp. and ed., *Mirando City: A New Town in a New Oil Field* (Laredo: Laredo Publishing Company, 1972), pp. 89–90.

8. Gunnar Brune, *Springs of Texas* (Fort Worth: Branch-Smith, Inc., 1981); Arturo Longoria, *Adios to the Brushlands* (College Station: Texas A&M University Press, 1997), p. 38.

9. Mary Anna Casstevens, "The Institution of the Spanish-Mexican Ranch and Its Culture in South Texas (Master's thesis, Texas A&M University-Kingsville, 1997), Chapter 1; Armando C. Alonzo, *Tejano Legacy: Rancheros and Settlers in South Texas, 1734–1900* (Albuquerque: University of New Mexico Press, 1998), pp. 74–75.

10. "Zapata Folklore," pp. 41–42; Lott, *Kingdom of Zapata*, p. 17; Hebbronville Chamber of Commerce, "Fiftieth Anniversary Jim Hogg County," pamphlet; Casstevens, "The Spanish-Mexican Ranch.

11. Domenech, *Missionary Adventures*, p. 273.

12. Florence Johnson Scott, *Historical Heritage of the Lower Rio Grande* (Waco: Texian Press, 1966), p. 131; Abel G. Rubio, *Stolen Heritage: A Mexican-American's Rediscovery of His Family's Lost Land Grant* (Austin: Eakin Press, 1986), p. 105.

13. Sister Mary Xavier, *Father Jaillet: Saddlebag Priest of the Nueces* (Corpus Christi: Diocese of Corpus Christi, 1948), pp. 20–26, 93; Alonzo, *Tejano Legacy*, p. 210.

14. Scott, *Lower Rio Grande*, pp. 101–105.

15. Ibid., p. 107.

16. Roberto M. Villareal, "The Mexican-American Vaqueros of the Kenedy Ranch: A Social History" (Master's thesis, Texas A&I University, 1972), pp. 9, 10, 16; Wilson M. Hudson, *The Healer of Los Olmos and Other Mexican Lore* (Dallas: Southern Methodist University Press, 1951), p. 20.

17. Alonzo, "Tejano Ranches," p. 60; Emilia Schunior Ramirez, *Ranch Life in Hidalgo County after 1850* (Edinburg: New Santander Press, n.d.), Section I, n.p.; McAllen, *Heritage Sampler*, pp. 61, 103; Evan Anders, *Boss Rule in South Texas: The Progressive Era* (Austin: The University of Texas Press, 1982), p. xv. (Note: Ramirez's book is divided into numbered sections but has no page numbers).

18. Alonzo, "Tejano Ranches," p. 60; Guerra, "Folklore," pp. 10–12; Dorothy Ostrom Worrell, "Rita Alderete de San Miguel was Pioneer Mother and Eagle Pass Business Executive," reprinted in *Eagle Pass Guide*, Centennial Edition (1949), n.p.

19. Lott, *Kingdom of Zapata*, pp. 36–40; McAllen, *Heritage Sampler*, pp. 75, 83, and 103; *Raymondville Chronicle*, November 6, 1961.

20. Xavier, *Father Jaillet*, p. 93 ; Alonzo, "Tejano Ranches," p. 62; Melinda Rankin, *Twenty Years Among the Mexicans: A Narrative of Missionary Labor* (Cincinnati: Chase & Hill, Publishers, 1875), p. 36; Jovita González, "Social Life in Cameron, Starr, and Zapata Counties" (Master's thesis, University of Texas at Austin, 1930), p. 11; V. W. Lehmann, *Forgotten Legions: Sheep in the Rio Grande Plain of Texas* (El Paso: Western Press, 1969), p. 1.

Chapter 2. Life in a Casa de Sillar

1. Guerra, "Folklore, p. 50.

2. Ibid., pp. 20, 62; Ramirez, *Ranch Life*, Section III; Domenech, *Missionary Adventures*, p. 229.

3. Guerra, "Folklore, p. 22.

4. Xavier, *Father Jaillet*, p. 20; Ramirez, *Ranch Life*, Section III; Joe S. Graham, *Hecho en Tejas: Texas-Mexican Folk Arts and Crafts* (Denton: University of North Texas Press, 1991), pp. 311, 312.

5. George, *Historic Architecture*, pp. 1, 53; Valley By-Liners, *Gift of the Rio: Story of Texas' Tropical Borderland* (Mission: Border Kingdom Press, 1975), p. 158; Texas Forest Service, *Famous Trees of Texas* (n.d.), p. 15.

6. Graham, *Hecho en Tejas*, p. 312; Guerra, "Folklore," p. 11; Zapata County Historical Society, "Zapata County Folklore," (unpublished booklet in Zapata County Museum, 1983), p. 47.

7. González, "Social Life, p. 68.

8. George, *Historic Architecture*, pp. 50, 51; Ramirez, *Ranch Life*, Section III; Domenech, *Missionary Adventures*, p. 327; Villareal, "Vaqueros," p. 54.

9. George, *Historic Architecture*, pp. 50, 51; Ramirez, *Ranch Life*, Sections II, III; Valley By-Liners, *Gift of the Rio*, p. 231.

10. Jovita González & Eve Raleigh, *Caballero: A Historical Novel*, ed. by José E. Limón and María Cotera (College Station: Texas A&M University Press, 1996), xxxviii.

11. Valley By-Liners, *Gift of the Rio*, pp. 237–238.

12. Ramirez, *Ranch Life*, Section III.

13. Xavier, *Father Jaillet*, p. 84.

14. George, *Historic Architecture*, p. 24; Ramirez, *Ranch Life*, Sections II, III; Villareal, "Vaqueros," pp. 52, 53; Graham, *Hecho en Tejas*, pp. 296–298; Xavier, *Father Jaillet*, p. 19.

15. Ramirez, *Ranch Life*, Section III; Villareal, "Vaqueros," p. 53; Graham, *Hecho en Tejas*, p. 297; Xavier, *Father Jaillet*, p. 85.

16. Valley By-Liners, *Gift of the Rio*, pp. 232–237.

17. Texas Forest Service, *Famous Trees*, p. 9.

18. Ramirez, *Ranch Life*, Section II; Mary Anna Casstevens, article in Graham, *Hecho en Tejas*, p. 315.

19. Ramirez, *Ranch Life*, Section XI.

20. Xavier, *Father Jaillet*, pp. 96–97; Guerra, "Folklore," p. 27; Guadalupe San Miguel, Jr., *Let All of Them Take Heed: Mexican Americans and the Campaign for Educational Equality in Texas, 1910–1981* (Austin: University of Texas Press, 1987), p. 12.

21. Villareal, "Vaqueros," p. 16; Guerra, "Folklore," pp. 13, 14.

22. George, *Historic Architecture,* p. 53; Xavier, *Father Jaillet,* pp. 93, 95; Valley By-Liners, *Gift of the Rio,* p. 61; Lott, *Kingdom of Zapata,* p. 7; McAllen, *Heritage Sampler,* p. 83.

23. Ramirez, *Ranch Life,* Section III; Villareal, "Vaqueros," p. 53; Xavier, *Father Jaillet,* p. 83; Zapata, "Folklore," p. 10; Domenech, *Missionary Adventures,* p. 359; Guerra, "Folklore," p. 69; Jovita González, "Social Life in Cameron, Starr, and Zapata Counties, "(Master's thesis, University of Texas at Austin, 1930), p. 61.

24. Ramirez, *Ranch Life,* Section III; *Father Jaillet,* pp. 65, 98; "De la Garza Family History" (unpublished, located in Vertical File in Rio Grande Valley Historical Collection, University of Texas–Pan American), n.p.; Domenech, *Missionary Adventures,* p. 255; Guerra, "Folklore," p. 69.

25. Ramirez, *Ranch Life,* Section III; "De la Garza Family History"; Domenech, *Missionary Adventures,* p. 279.

26. Hebbronville Chamber of Commerce, "Fiftieth Anniversary Jim Hogg County," n.p.; Valley By-Liners, *Gift of the Rio,* p. 234.

27. Ibid.; Guerra, "Folklore," p. 112; Lott, *Kingdom of Zapata,* p. 45.

Chapter 3. Primos *and* Compadres *Across the Frontier*

1. U.S. Census of Population, Tenth Census of the United States: 1880. Cameron, Starr, and Hidalgo Counties, Texas *MSS.*

2. Ramirez, *Ranch Life,* Section I.

3. Guerra, "Folklore," p. 58; Domenech, *Missionary Adventures,* p. 255; Paredes, *With His Pistol in His Hand,* p. 13.

4. John D. Eisenhower, *So Far from God: The U.S. War with Mexico, 1846–1848* (New York: Anchor Books, 1990), p. 103; Domenech, *Missionary Adventures,* pp. 255–56, 289.

5. Guerra, "Folklore," pp. 19–20; Paredes, *With His Pistol in His Hand,* p. 11; Villareal, "Vaqueros," p. 56.

6. Guerra, "Folklore," pp. 64, 65.

7. Worrell, "Rita Alderete de San Miguel."

8. Paredes, *With His Pistol in His Hand,* p. 12.

9. George, *Historic Architecture,* p. 36.

10. Ramirez, *Ranch Life,* Section III.

11. Graham, *Hecho en Tejas,* p. 15, figure 4; Domenech, *Missionary Adventures,* p. 38; Guerra, "Folklore," p. 30.

12. Guerra, "Folklore," pp. 22–25.

13. Ramirez, *Ranch Life,* Section III; Paredes, *With His Pistol in His Hand,* p. 12.

14. Guerra, "Folklore," pp. 66, 67; U.S. Census of Population, Tenth Census of the United States: 1880. Cameron, Starr, and Hidalgo Counties, Texas *MSS;* U.S. Census of Population, Seventh Census of the United States, 1850, *MSS.*

15. Lott, *Kingdom of Zapata,* p. 25.

16. Ibid.

17. Ramirez, *Ranch Life,* Section IX; Guerra, "Folklore," pp. 92, 112; Domenech, *Missionary Adventures,* pp. 256, 278; Xavier, *Father Jaillet,* p. 21.

18. Domenech, *Missionary Adventures,* pp. 278, 325.

19. Paredes, *With His Pistol in His Hand,* p. 13.

20. Guha, *Elementary Aspects of Peasant Insurgency;* Edward Countryman, *The American Revolution* (New York: Hill and Wang, 1985), p. 61; Ramirez, *Ranch Life,* Section I.

Chapter 4. The Art and Skills of Tejano Life

1. Ramirez, *Ranch Life,* Section IV.
2. Guerra, "Folklore," pp. 46, 69, 70.
3. Mari Sandoz, *The Cattlemen: From the Rio Grande Across the Far Marias* (Lincoln: University of Nebraska Press, 1978), p. 104; Kathleen Mullen Sands, *Charrería Mexicana: An Equestrian Folk Tradition* (Tucson: The University of Arizona Press, 1993), pp. 41, 42; Guerra, "Folklore," pp. 46.
4. Villareal, "Vaqueros," pp. 41, 42, 46; Domenech, *Missionary Adventures,* p. 100; Ricardo M. Beasley, Beasley Manuscripts, Estate of R. M. Beasley, plate 8.
5. Villareal, "Vaqueros," p. 47; Sands, *Charrería Mexicana,* pp. 45, 46, 109, 110; Beasley, Beasley Manuscripts, plate 4.
6. Sandoz, *The Cattlemen,* pp. 104, 105.
7. Villareal, "Vaqueros," p. 21; Beasley, Beasley Manuscripts, plate 5.
8. Joe S. Graham, *El Rancho in South Texas: Continuity and Change from 1750* (Denton: University of North Texas Press, 1994), p. 26; Guerra, "Folklore," p. 63; Domenech, *Missionary Adventures,* p. 309; Paredes, *With His Pistol in His Hand,* p. 10.
9. Guerra, "Folklore," p. 59.
10. Carey McWilliams, *North from Mexico: The Spanish-Speaking People of the United States* (New York: Greenwood Press, 1970), p. 149.
11. Guerra, "Folklore," pp. 57, 58; V. W. Lehmann, *Forgotten Legions: Sheep in the Rio Grande Plain of Texas* (El Paso: Western Press, 1969), p. 57.
12. Frederick Law Olmsted, *Journey Through Texas: Or A Saddletrip on the Southwestern Frontier: With a Statistical Appendix* (New York: Dix, Edwards & Co., 1857), p. 162; Agnes G. Grimm, *Llanos Mestenas: Mustang Plains* (Waco: Texian Press, 1968), p. 43.
13. Texas, *State Gazette Appendix,* Vol. II, No. 6, Box 100-1497, RG 100, Legislative Records (Archives, Texas State Library).
14. Valley By-Liners, *Gift of the Rio,* p. 169.
15. Olmsted, *Journey Through Texas,* p. 162.
16. Valley By-Liners, *Gift of the Rio,* pp. 95, 168, 233, 234; Robertson, *Wild Horse Desert,* p. 89.
17. Guerra, "Folklore," pp. 15, 21, 25.
18. Domenech, *Missionary Adventures,* p. 217.
19. Grimm, *Llanos Mestenas,* p. 30; Valley By-Liners, *Gift of the Rio,* p. 169; Domenech, *Missionary Adventures,* p. 225; George, *Historic Architecture,* p. 25; Ramirez, *Ranch Life,* Section IV; William A. McClintock, "Journal of a Trip through Texas and Northern Mexico in 1846–1847," *Southwestern Historical Quarterly* 34 (1930–31): 241.
20. Zapata, "Folklore," p. 46.
21. Hidalgo County, Court Record Book A, pp. 3–18; Robertson, *Wild Horse Desert,* p. 90; Valley By-Liners, *Gift of the Rio,* p. 231.

Chapter 5. Tejano Culture at Work and Play

1. Peña, *Texas-Mexican Conjunto,* p. 11; Domenech, *Missionary Adventures,* p. 256.
2. Domenech, *Missionary Adventures,* pp. 257, 288.
3. Villareal, "Vaqueros," p. 34.
4. Guadalupe San Miguel, Jr., *Let All of Them Take Heed: Mexican Americans and the Campaign for Educational Equality in Texas, 1910–1981* (Austin: University of Texas Press, 1987), pp. 8, 9.

5. Ibid., pp. 8, 9, 12; Hinojosa, *Hinojosa Family,* pp. 8–10; Xavier, *Father Jaillet,* p. 6; González, "Social Life, p. 69.

6. González, "Social Life, p. 107.

7. Ramirez, *Ranch Life,* Section XI; Xavier, *Father Jaillet,* pp. 96–97; Guerra, "Folklore," pp. 38, 39; Lott, *Kingdom of Zapata,* p. 100.

8. Paredes, *With His Pistol in His Hand,* p. 14; Xavier, *Father Jaillet,* p. 101; Domenech, *Missionary Adventures,* p. 306.

9. Guerra, "Folklore," pp. 72–100.

10. Ibid., pp. 92, 93; Lehmann, *Forgotten Legions,* p. 63.

11. Guerra, "Folklore," pp. 54, 80, 97; Valley By-Liners, *Gift of the Rio,* p. 238.

12. Domenech, *Missionary Adventures,* p. 257; Guerra, "Folklore," p. 124; Beasley, Beasley Manuscripts, plate 21.

13. Guerra, "Folklore," pp. 86–88.

14. *Raymondville Chronicle,* November 6, 1961; Richard R. Flores, *Los Pastores: History and Performance in the Mexican Shepherd's Play of South Texas* (Washington: Smithsonian Institution Press, 1995); Villareal, "Vaqueros," p. 63; Guerra, "Folklore," pp. 112–18, 129–37.

15. Zapata, "Folklore," pp. 47, 52; Ramirez, *Ranch Life,* Section XI; Guerra, "Folklore," pp. 119–29.

16. Villareal, "Vaqueros," p. 122.

17. Peña, *Texas-Mexican Conjunto,* pp. 38, 47.

18. González, "Social Life, pp. 53, 54; Domenech, *Missionary Adventures,* p. 277; Xavier, *Father Jaillet,* p. 92; Villareal, "Vaqueros," pp. 22, 56; Celso Garza Guajardo, *En busca de Catarino Garza, 1859–1895* (Monterrey: Universidad Autónoma de Nuevo León, 1989), p. 70.

Chapter 6. A Tejano Prayer

1. Timothy M. Matovina, *Tejano Religion and Ethnicity: San Antonio, 1821–1860* (Austin: University of Texas Press, 1995), p. 17.

2. Jackson Ranch File, Rio Grande Historical Collection (University of Texas–Pan American), pp. 1, 13; McAllen, *Heritage Sampler,* p. 83; R. Douglas Brackenridge and Francisco O. Garcia-Treto, *Iglesia Presbiteriana: A History of Presbyterians and Mexican Americans in the Southwest* (San Antonio: Trinity University Press, 1974), p. 10; Valley By-Liners, *Gift of the Rio,* pp. 152, 173; Texas Garden Clubs, *History Trail on the Rio Grande,* booklet (Texas Garden Clubs, Inc., n.d.), n.p.; Robertson, *Wild Horse Desert,* p. 93; Xavier, *Father Jaillet,* p. 2.

3. Xavier, *Father Jaillet,* p. 26; Domenech, *Missionary Adventures,* pp. 278, 279; Valley By-Liners, *Gift of the Rio,* pp. 152–56, 173; Matovina, *Tejano Religion,* p. 14.

4. Xavier, *Father Jaillet,* p. 18; Domenech, *Missionary Adventures,* p. 3.

5. Matovina, *Tejano Religion,* p. 67; Brackenridge, *Iglesia Presbiteriana,* p. 13; Xavier, *Father Jaillet,* pp. 93, 110, 210; Rankin, *Twenty Years,* p. 36.

6. El Capote Ranch File, Rio Grande Historical Collection, University of Texas–Pan American, p. 1; Jackson Ranch File, pp. 1, 4, 13; Hidalgo County, Court Record Book A, p. 48; Walter W. Hildebrand, "The History of Cameron County, Texas (Master's thesis, North Texas State College, 1950), p. 26; Guerra, "Folklore," p. 27; Lott, *Kingdom of Zapata,* p. 7; Valley By-Liners, *Rio Grande Roundup,* p. 61; Xavier, *Father Jaillet,* pp. 93, 95; Graham, *Hecho en Tejas,* p. 316; George, *Historic Architecture,* p. 59; Zapata, "Folklore," pp. 41, 42; Beasley, Beasley Manuscripts, plate 17.

7. George, *Historic Architecture*, p. 75; Xavier, *Father Jaillet*, p. 46; Guerra, "Folklore," p. 22; Valley By-Liners, *Gift of the Rio*, p. 232.

8. González, *Caballero*, pp. 3–6.

9. Xavier, *Father Jaillet*, p. 21; Guerra, "Folklore," p. 17; Zapata, "Folklore," p. 47; González, "Social Life, p. 68.

10. Guerra, "Folklore," pp. 20, 28, 30.

11. Domenech, *Missionary Adventures*, p. 358.

12. Xavier, *Father Jaillet*, pp. 21, 98; Ramirez, *Ranch Life*, Section VI.

13. Xavier, *Father Jaillet*, pp. 92, 93; Domenech, *Missionary Adventures*, 259; Guerra, "Folklore," p. 26

14. Xavier, *Father Jaillet*, pp. 26, 30.

15. Jean Louis Berlandier, *Journey to Mexico During the Years 1826 to 1834*, 2 vols. (Austin: Texas State Historical Association, 1980), 2: 429; Valley By-Liners, *Gift of the Rio*, p. 202.

16. Guerra, "Folklore," p. 67; Matovina, *Tejano Religion*, p. 67; Domenech, *Missionary Adventures*, pp. 259, 287.

17. Wilson M. Hudson, *The Healer of Los Olmos and Other Mexican Lore* (Dallas: Southern Methodist University Press, 1951), p. 12.

Epilogue: A Legacy of Heritage and Conflict

1. Texas General Land Office, *Abstract of All Original Texas Land Titles Comprising Grants and Locations to August 31, 1942*, 8 vols. (Austin: The State of Texas, 1942); Texas, *State Gazette Appendix*, Vol. II, No. 6; Rubio, *Stolen Heritage*, p. 115. For a more detailed analysis of the statistical data in the Tejano land and census records, see Andrew A. Tijerina, "Tejanos and Texas: The Native Mexicans of Texas, 1820–1850" (Ph.D. diss., University of Texas, 1977), Chapter VII.

2. Bruce S. Cheeseman, "Richard King: Pioneering Market Capitalism on the Frontier, in Graham, *Ranching in South Texas*, p. 88.

3. *Informe de La Comisión Pesquisidora*, pp. 18, 19, 68; Hidalgo County, Court Record Book A, p. 149.

4. *Informe de La Comisión Pesquisidora*, 106; Octavio Herrera Perez, *Monografía de Reynosa* (Tamaulipas, México: Instituto Tamaulipeco de Cultura, 1989), p. 68.

5. J. B. (Red) Dunn, *Perilous Trails of Texas*, ed. by Lilith Lorraine (Dallas: Southwest Press, 1932), pp. 9, 63.

6. Ibid., pp. 36, 41.

7. Villareal, "Vaqueros," pp. 16–19.

8. John C. Rayburn and Virginia Kemp Rayburn, eds., with the assistance of Ethel Neale Fry, *Century of Conflict, 1821–1913: Incidents in the Lives of William Neale and William A. Neale, Early Settlers in South Texas* (Waco: Texian Press, 1966), pp. 103–106; Walter Prescott Webb, *The Texas Rangers: A Century of Frontier Defense*, 2d ed. (Austin: University of Texas Press, 1991), p. 238; Villareal, "Vaqueros," pp. 16–19; Montejano, *Anglos and Mexicans*, p. 53.

9. Villareal, "Vaqueros," pp. 16–19.

10. Paredes, *With His Pistol in His Hand*, p. 28.

11. Dunn, *Perilous Trails of Texas*, pp. 36, 41; Domenech, *Missionary Adventures*, p. 177; Webb, *Texas Rangers*, p. 227.

12. Alonzo, *Tejano Legacy*, p. 138; Guerra, "Folklore," p. 138.

13. Arthur J. Rubel, *Across the Tracks: Mexican-Americans in a Texas City* (Austin: University of Texas Press, 1966), p. 36.

14. Guerra, "Folklore," pp. 41–44.

15. Webb, *Texas Rangers*, p. 463.

16. Villareal, "Vaqueros," pp. 7, 10; Montejano, *Anglos and Mexicans*, p. 69; Ana Caroline Castillo Crimm, "Success in Adversity: The Mexican Americans of Victoria County, Texas, 1800–1880" (Ph.D. diss., University of Texas at Austin, 1994), pp. 8, 174, 187.

17. Guerra, "Folklore," p. 138.

18. Alonzo, *Tejano Legacy*, p. 11; Douglas K. Boyd, Andrés Tijerina, Karl W. Kibler, Amy C. Earl, and Martha Doty Freeman, "Pharr-Reynosa International Bridge: Continued Archeological and Historical Research at El Capote Ranch Community, Hidalgo County, Texas, *Reports of Investigation No. 97* (Austin: Texas Antiquities Committee, 1994), pp. 33, 38.

19. Walter Prescott Webb, *The Great Plains* (New York: Grosset & Dunlap, 1931), p. 209. For demography, see Arnoldo De León and Kenneth L. Stewart, *Tejanos and the Numbers Game: A Socio-Historical Interpretation from the Federal Census, 1850–1900* (Albuquerque: University of New Mexico Press, 1989), which set Tejano population figures for South Texas counties at 9,888 by 1880; and Terry G. Jordan, *Trails to Texas: Southern Roots of Western Cattle Ranching* (Lincoln: University of Nebraska Press, 1981), p. 151, who argues that Mexican ranching had "disappeared before 1850 in the South Texas region between San Antonio and the Rio Grande, leaving only insignigicant numbers of ranches after that year."

20. U.S. Congress, House of Representatives, *Difficulties on Southwestern Frontier*, Ex. Doc. No. 52, 36th Cong., 1st sess., 1860, pp. 70–72.

21. Texas, *State Gazette Appendix*, Vol. II, No. 6.

22. Matovina, *Tejano Religion*, p. 78.

23. Evan Anders, *Boss Rule in South Texas: The Progressive Era* (Austin: University of Texas Press, 1982), pp. 268, 271, 272; Webb, *Texas Rangers*, pp. 515, 516.

24. For a full description of this resistance paradigm, see James C. Scott, *Domination and the Arts of Resistance*.

25. Rubio, *Stolen Heritage*, pp. 172, 173.

GLOSSARY

aguador (ah-wah-dor), a water carrier

ahijada (a-ee-ha-da), goddaughter

ahijado (a-ee-ha-do), godson

albañiles, brickmasons

aljibe (al-hee-beh), cistern

almuerzo (al-mwer-so), a heavier midmorning breakfast

el altarcito (al-tar-see-toh), household altar

anacahuita (anna-ka-weeta), wild olive

anacua (an-ak-wa), an evergreen tree

"Arre, arre" (ar-ray, ar-ray)

arrieros (ar-ree-air-ros), mule drivers

bajío (ba-hee-oh)

braza, ember

buque (boo-ke), a large rawhide tub

cabañuelas (ca-ban-weh-las), a complicated traditional almanac calculation for meteorological observations

cabeza de silla (ka-bess-ah de see-ya), literally "saddle head," the saddle horn

cabresto (ca-bress-tow), a handmade horsehair rope

canales (ca-na-less), downspouts for water

la canícula (kah-nee-coo-la), the solstices and the phases of the moon

la capilla (ka-pee-ya), chapel

caporal (ka-po-ral), team leader

carpinteros, carpenters

carreteros (car-re-ter-ros), cart drivers

cascarrones (kas-ka-ron-ess), confetti-filled eggshells

El Caudal (cow-dal), a parlor game

La Cautiva (cow-tee-va),

chalan (cha-lawn), a ferry

chicharrones (chee-cha-ron-ess), cracklings

chicote (chee-ko-teh), a bullwhip

chorrear (chor-yar), spinning action

ciprés (see-press), bald cypress

cocinero (ko-see-neh-roh), the cook

comadre (co-mod-re), co-mother

compadrazgo (com-pad-ross-ko), godparenting

compadre (com-pod-re), co-father

convite (con-vee-teh), the formal wedding invitation

corrida (kor-ree-dah), a team

cortar (kor-tar), cutting animals from the herd

cubeta (koo-bet-ta), a wooden bucket for a well

curandero (koor-an-deh-roh), a folk healer

dale vuelta (da-le-wel-ta), to tie a single turn around the saddle horn

descanso (dess-can-so), "rest"

deshilado (dess-ee-lah-doh), drawnwork

despoblado (dess-pob-la-doh), depopulated zone

la diligencia (la dee-lee-hen-see-ya), stage line

doña (don-ya)

esquifa (ess-kee-fah), a skiff

estranjero, foreigner

frijoles (free-ho-less)

el frijolillo (free-ho-lee-yo), Texas mountain laurel

galones (gah-lo-ness), decorative metal disks

guajillo (wa-hee-yo), a native Texas shrub

guaripa (wa-ree-pa), a large cowhide used to draw heavy loads behind a team of draft animals

horcones (or-ko-ness), corner posts of a jacal

horno (orr-no), dome-shaped outdoor oven

"J" (ho-tah)

jacal (ha-kal)

el jazmin (hass-meen), white flowering jasmine

jinetear (hee-ne-te-ar), breaking a bronc

Jotena (ho-te-nah)

lajas (la-hass)

lanero, a boy who gathers shorn wool

lasar (la-sarr), to rope

lavanderas, laundrywomen

Lechusa (leh-chu-sah), a witch

llovediza (yo-veh-dee-sa), dew/rainwater stored in a cistern

madrina, godmother

mangana, throwing a rope loop around a running animal's forelegs

mangana a pie (ah-pyeh), throwing a loop from a standing position

manzeador (mon-say-ah-dor), an expert specialized in bronc busting

mayordomo, ranch foreman

mecapal (me-ka-pal), a burlap bundle carried on the back and supported with a long strap looped around their forehead

menudo (meh-noo-dow), a soup from a beef stomach

merienda (mer-yen-da) snack

metate (me-tot-tay), a large grinding mortar

migas (mee-gass), tortilla chips in egg dish

molcajete (mol-ka-het-tay), a small grinding mortar

molinillo (mo-leen-ee-yo), a wooden hand blender

Las Mujeres (moo-hair-ess), women

nopalitos (no-pa-lee-tos), edible tender cactus leaves

noria (nor-ya), a water well

ojarasca (oh-ha-ross-ka), wedding cookie

ojo (o-ho), natural springs

Ojuelos (oh-whel-ohs)

Ortiguilla (or-tee-gee-ya), weed
padrino, godfather
partida (par-tee-dah), cattle drive
Peñascal (pen-yass-kal)
pial (pyal), throwing a loop around the hind legs
piloncillo (pee-lon-cee-yo), a Mexican candy
porción (por-se-on)
el portal (por-tall), a patio roof structure
presa (press-ah), an earthen dam
primo (pree-mo), cousin
punteo (poon-tay-oh), needlework
rejas (reh-has), wrought iron bars
remudero (re-moo-deh-roh), a young workers, usually around age 10 to 14, who tended the
    spare horses
revoque (re-vo-keh), a grass and mortar mixture for walls
rinches (reen-chess), Rangers
robavacas (ro-ba-va-kas), cattle rustlers
salarete (sal-a-re-te), baking soda
Santiaguero (san-tee-ah-ger-oh)
segundo (se-goon-doh), second in command
sillar (see-yar)
tambora de rancho (tam-bo-rah), a large drum
taquito (ta-kee-tow)
tasinques (ta-seen-kess), sheep shearers
"Tildio" (teel-dee-o), a plover's song
la trasquila (tras-kee-la), sheep shearing
troneras (tro-ner-ahs)
tule (too-leh), bull rushes
turcos (toor-koss), a baked mince pie of spiced pork loin with cinnamon, sugar, nuts, and
    raisins
vado (vah-doh), a river ford
la velación (veh-lah-see-on), the formal wedding ceremony conducted by a priest
vigas (vee-goss), massive, wooden roof beams
zacahuixtle (saka-weeks-leh), a long-stemmed grass; zacaton
zarzo (sar-so), a flat, square cheese rack

BIBLIOGRAPHY

Alonzo, Armando C. "Change and Continuity in Tejano Ranches in the Trans-Nueces, 1848–
1900." In Joe S. Graham, *Proceedings of "Ranching in South Texas: A Symposium."*
Kingsville: Texas A&M University–Kingsville, 1994.

———. *Tejano Legacy: Rancheros and Settlers in South Texas, 1734–1900.* Albuquerque:
University of New Mexico Press, 1998.

Anders, Evan. *Boss Rule in South Texas: The Progressive Era.* Austin: The University of Texas
Press, 1982.

Arnold, August. *The Folklore, Manners and Customs of the Mexican Americans in San Antonio,
Texas.* Austin: The University of Texas Press, 1928.

Bailey, Ben P., Jr. *Border Lands Sketchbook.* Waco: Texian Press, 1976.

Bauer, K. Jack. *The Mexican War, 1846–1848.* Lincoln: University of Nebraska Press, 1974.

Beasley, Ricardo M. Beasley Manuscripts. R. M. Beasley Estate.

Bello Lopez, Leopoldo. *Platicame algo de un vaquero.* Ciudad Victoria: Instituto Tamaulipeco
de Cultura, 1990.

Berlandier, Jean Louis. *Journey to Mexico During the Years 1826 to 1834.* 2 vols. Austin: Texas
State Historical Association, 1980.

Black, F. Michael, comp. and ed. *Mirando City: A New Town in a New Oil Field.* Laredo:
Laredo Publishing Company, 1972.

Blassingame, John W. *The Slave Community: Plantation Life in the Antebellum South.* New
York: Oxford University Press, 1972.

Boyd, Douglas K., Andrés Tijerina, Karl W. Kibler, Amy C. Earl, and Martha Doty
Freeman. "Pharr-Reynosa International Bridge: Continued Archeological and Historical
Research at El Capote Ranch Community, Hidalgo County, Texas." *Reports of Investiga-
tion No. 97.* Austin: Texas Antiquities Committee, 1994.

Brackenridge, R. Douglas, and Francisco O. García-Treto. *Iglesia Presbiteriana: A History of
Presbyterians and Mexican Americans in the Southwest.* San Antonio: Trinity University
Press, 1974.

Brown, Mark Herbert. *Before Barbed Wire.* New York: Holt, 1956.

Brune, Gunnar. *Springs of Texas.* Fort Worth: Branch-Smith, Inc., 1981.

Casstevens, Mary Anna. "The Institution of the Spanish-Mexican Ranch and Its Culture in
South Texas." Master's thesis, Texas A&M University–Kingsville, 1997.

Cavness, Addie Word. *La Puerta de Agua Dulce: A Chronicle of the Everyday Life of a Ranch
Family Circa 1895–1913.* Austin: Shelby Printing, 1973.

Cheeseman, Bruce S. "Richard King: Pioneering Market Capitalism on the Frontier." In Joe
S. Graham, *Proceedings of "Ranching in South Texas: A Symposium."* Kingsville: Texas
A&M University–Kingsville, 1994.

Countryman, Edward. *The American Revolution.* New York: Hill and Wang, 1985.

Covian Martinez, Vidal Efren. *Compendio de historia de Tamaulipas.* Ciudad Victoria:
Ediciones Siglo XX, 1973.

Dale, Edward Everett. *Frontier Ways: Sketches of Life in the Old West.* Austin: University of Texas Press, 1959.

De León, Arnoldo. *Apuntes Tejanos.* Ann Arbor: University Microfilms International, 1978.

———. *The Tejano Community, 1836–1900.* Albuquerque: University of New Mexico Press, 1982.

De León, Arnoldo, and Kenneth L. Stewart. *Tejanos and the Numbers Game: A Socio-Historical Interpretation from the Federal Census, 1850–1900.* Albuquerque: University of New Mexico Press, 1989.

Dobie, J. Frank. *A Vaquero of the Brush Country.* Dallas: Southwest Press, 1929.

Domenech, Abbé. *Missionary Adventures in Texas and Mexico: A Personal Narrative of Six Years' Sojourn in Those Regions.* London: Longman, Brown, Green, Longmans, and Roberts, 1858.

Dunn, J. B. (Red). *Perilous Trails of Texas.* Edited by Lilith Lorraine. Dallas: Southwest Press, 1932.

Eisenhower, John D. *So Far from God: The U.S. War with Mexico, 1846–1848.* New York: Anchor Books, 1990.

El Capote Ranch File. Rio Grande Historical Collection, University of Texas-Pan American.

Fish, Jean Y. *José Vasquez Borrego and La Hacienda de Nuestra Señora de Dolores.* Zapata, Texas: Zapata County Historical Society, 1991.

García, Mario T. *Mexican Americans: Leadership, Ideology, & Identity, 1930–1960.* New Haven: Yale University Press, 1989.

Garza Guajardo, Celso. *En busca de Catarino Garza, 1859–1895.* Monterrey: Universidad Autónoma de Nuevo León, 1989.

George, Eugene. *The Historic Architecture of Texas: The Falcón Reservoir.* Austin: Texas Historical Commission, 1975.

Gómez-Quiõnes, Juan. *Roots of Chicano Politics, 1600–1940.* Albuquerque: University of New Mexico Press, 1994.

Gonzalez, Arturo. *Historia de Tamaulipas.* 2d ed. Ciudad Victoria: Libreria "El Lapiz rojo," 1931.

González, Jovita, & Eve Raleigh. *Caballero: A Historical Novel.* Edited by José E. Limón and María Cotera. College Station: Texas A&M University Press, 1996.

González, Jovita. "Social Life in Cameron, Starr, and Zapata Counties." Master's thesis, University of Texas at Austin, 1930.

Goodwyn, Frank. *Life on the King Ranch.* New York: Crowell, 1951.

Graham, Joe S. *El Rancho in South Texas: Continuity and Change from 1750.* Denton: University of North Texas Press, 1994.

———. *Hecho en Tejas: Texas-Mexican Folk Arts and Crafts.* Denton: University of North Texas Press, 1991.

———. *Proceedings of "Ranching in South Texas: A Symposium."* Kingsville: Texas A&M University-Kingsville, 1994.

Greaser, Galen D., and Jesús de la Teja. "Quieting Title to Spanish and Mexican Land Grants in the Trans-Nueces: The Bourland and Miller Commission, 1850–1852." *Southwestern Historical Quarterly* 95, no. 4 (April, 1992): 445–64.

Grimm, Agnes G. *Llanos Mestenas: Mustang Plains.* Waco: Texian Press, 1968.

Guerra, Fermina. "Mexican and Spanish Folklore and Incidents in Southwest Texas." Master's thesis, University of Texas, 1941.

Guha, Ranajit. *Elementary Aspects of Peasant Insurgency in Colonial India.* Delhi: Oxford University Press, 1983.

Harper, Minnie Timms. *Old Ranches.* Dallas: Dealey and Lowe, 1936.

Hebbronville Chamber of Commerce. "Fiftieth Anniversary Jim Hogg County." Pamphlet, n.d. Unpublished booklet, 1963.

Herrera Perez, Octavio. *Monografía de Reynosa.* Tamaulipas, México: Instituto Tamaulipeco de Cultura, 1989.

Hidalgo County. Court Record Book A.

Hill, Lawrence F. *José de Escandon and the Founding of Nuevo Santander: A Study in Spanish Colonization.* Columbus: Ohio State University Press, 1926.

Hinojosa, Alicia. *The Hinojosa Family: From Mier, Tamaulipas, Mexico to Texas.* Utica, Kansas: McDowell Publications, 1992.

Hudson, Wilson M. *The Healer of Los Olmos and Other Mexican Lore.* Dallas: Southern Methodist University Press, 1951.

Jackson Ranch File. Rio Grande Historical Collection, University of Texas–Pan American.

Jackson, Jack. *Los Mesteños: Spanish Ranching in Texas, 1721–1821.* College Station: Texas A&M University Press, 1986.

Jordan, Terry G. *Trails to Texas: Southern Roots of Western Cattle Ranching.* Lincoln: University of Nebraska Press, 1981.

Kearney, Milo. *Studies in Brownsville History.* Brownsville: Pan American University at Brownsville, 1986.

Kendall, George Wilkins. *Letters from a Texas Sheep Ranch, Written in the Years 1860 and 1867.* Urbana: University of Illinois Press, 1959.

Lamar, Mirabeau B. *Papers of Mirabeau Buonaparte Lamar.* 6 vols. Austin: A. C. Baldwin and Sons, [1921–27].

Lehmann, V. W. *Forgotten Legions; Sheep in the Rio Grande Plain of Texas.* El Paso: Western Press, 1969.

Longoria, Arturo. *Adios to the Brushlands.* College Station: Texas A&M University Press, 1997.

Los Caminos del Rio Heritage Project. *A Shared Experience: The History, Architecture and Historic Designations of the Lower Rio Grande Heritage Corridor.* Austin: Texas Historical Commission, 1994.

Lott, Virgil N., and Mercurio Martinez. *The Kingdom of Zapata.* San Antonio: The Naylor Company, 1953.

McAllen, Margaret. *The Heritage Sampler: Selections from the Rich and Colorful History of the Rio Grande Valley.* Edinburg: New Sandander Press, 1991.

Maril, Robert Lee. *Living on the Edge of America: At Home on the Texas-Mexico Border.* College Station: Texas A&M University Press, 1992.

Matovina, Timothy M. *Tejano Religion and Ethnicity: San Antonio, 1821–1860.* Austin: University of Texas Press, 1995.

McClintock, William A. "Journal of a Trip through Texas and Northern Mexico in 1846–1847." *Southwestern Historical Quarterly* 34 (1930–31): 20-37, 141–58, and 231–56.

McLean, R. N. *That Mexican! As He Really Is North and South of the Rio Grande.* New York: Fleming H. Revell Co., 1928.

McWilliams, Carey. *North from Mexico: The Spanish-Speaking People of the United States.* New York: Greenwood Press, 1970.

México. *Informe de La Comisión Pesquisidora de la Frontera del Norte al Ejecutivo de la Union.* Monterrey: Imprenta de Diaz de Leon y White, 1874.

Montejano, David. *Anglos and Mexicans in the Making of Texas, 1836–1886.* Austin: University of Texas Press, 1987.

———. *Race, Labor Repression, and Capitalist Agriculture: Notes from South Texas, 1920–1930.* Berkeley: Institute for the Study of Social Change, 1977.

Moore, Ben. *Random Shots and Tales of Texas.* Seagraves, Texas: Pioneer Book Publishers, 1977.

Olmsted, Frederick Law. *Journey Through Texas: Or A Saddletrip on the Southwestern Frontier: With a Statistical Appendix.* New York: Dix, Edwards & Co., 1857.

Paredes, Américo. *Folklore and Culture on the Texas-Mexican Border.* Austin: Center for Mexican American Studies, 1993.

———. *With His Pistol in His Hand: A Border Ballad and Its Hero.* Austin: University of Texas Press, 1958.

Peavy, John R. *Echoes from the Rio Grande, 1905 to Now.* Brownsville, Texas: Springman-King Co., 1963.

Peña, Manuel. *The Texas-Mexican Conjunto: History of a Working-Class Music.* Austin: University of Texas Press, 1985.

Pierce, Frank C. *A Brief History of the Lower Rio Grande Valley.* Menasha, Wis.: George Banta Publishing Company, 1917.

Ramirez, Elizabeth C. *Footlights Across the Border: A History of Spanish Language Professional Theater on the Texas Stage.* New York: P. Lang, 1990.

Ramirez, Emilia Schunior. *Ranch Life in Hidalgo County after 1850.* Edinburg: New Santander Press, n.d.

Ramsey, Closner. "Scrapbook of the Lower Rio Grande Valley." Manuscript belonging to Eugene George.

Rankin, Melinda. *Twenty Years Among the Mexicans: A Narrative of Missionary Labor.* Cincinnati: Chase & Hill, Publishers, 1875.

Rayburn, John C., and Virginia Kemp Rayburn, eds., with the assistance of Ethel Neale Fry. *Century of Conflict, 1821–1913: Incidents in the Lives of William Neale and William A. Neale, Early Settlers in South Texas.* Waco: Texian Press, 1966.

Raymondville, *Raymondville Chronicle.* Raymondville, Texas.

Robertson, Brian. *Wild Horse Desert: The Heritage of South Texas.* Edinburg: New Santander Press, 1985.

Rojas, Arnold R. *The Vaquero.* Charlotte, N.C.: McNally and Loftin, 1964.

Rubel, Arthur J. *Across the Tracks: Mexican-Americans in a Texas City.* Austin: University of Texas Press, 1966.

Rubio, Abel G. *Stolen Heritage: A Mexican-American's Rediscovery of His Family's Lost Land Grant.* Austin: Eakin Press, 1986.

Samponaro, Frank N., and Paul J. Vanderwood. *War Scare on the Rio Grande: Robert Runyon's Photographs of the Border Conflict, 1913–1916.* Austin: Texas State Historical Association, 1992.

San Miguel, Guadalupe, Jr. *Let All of Them Take Heed: Mexican Americans and the Campaign for Educational Equality in Texas, 1910–1981.* Austin: University of Texas Press, 1987.

Sandoz, Mari. *The Cattlemen: From the Rio Grande Across the Far Marias.* Lincoln: University of Nebraska Press, 1978.

Sands, Kathleen Mullen. *Charrería Mexicana: An Equestrian Folk Tradition.* Tucson: The University of Arizona Press, 1993.

Scott, Florence Johnson. *Historical Heritage of the Lower Rio Grande.* Waco: Texian Press, 1966.

Scott, James C. *Domination and the Arts of Resistance: Hidden Transcripts.* New Haven: Yale University Press, 1990.

Sloss-Vento, Adela. *Alonso S. Perales: His Struggle for the Rights of Mexican-Americans.* San Antonio: Artes Graficas, 1977.

State Gazette Appendix. Legislative Records. Texas State Library Archives.

Texas Forest Service. *Famous Trees of Texas.* N.d.

Texas Garden Clubs. "History Trail on the Rio Grande." Booklet. Texas Garden Clubs, Inc., n.d.

Texas. General Land Office. "Report of James R. Miller & W. H. Bourland, Commissioners to Investigate Land Titles West of the Nueces." *MSS.* 1854.

———. *Abstract of All Original Texas Land Titles Comprising Grants and Locations to August 31, 1942.* 8 vols. Austin: The State of Texas, 1942.

Tijerina, Andrés. *Tejanos and Texas under the Mexican Flag, 1821–1836.* College Station: Texas A&M University Press, 1994.

Tijerina, Andrew A. "Tejanos and Texas: The Native Mexicans of Texas, 1820–1850." Ph.D. diss., University of Texas, Austin, 1977.

U.S. Congress, House of Representatives. *Difficulties on Southwestern Frontier.* Ex. Doc. No. 52. 36th Cong., 1st sess., 1860.

U.S. Census of Population. The Seventh Census of the United States: 1850. Texas. *MSS* (microfilm).

U.S. Census of Population. The Tenth Census of the United States: 1880. Cameron, Starr, and Hidalgo Counties, Texas. *MSS.*

U.S. Department of State. Proceedings of the International Water Boundary Commission. 2 vols. Washington, D.C.: U.S. Government Printing Office, 1893.

Valley By-Liners. *Gift of the Rio: Story of Texas' Tropical Borderland.* Mission: Border Kingdom Press, 1975.

———. *Rio Grande Roundup: Story of Texas' Tropical Borderlands.* Mission: Border Kingdom Press, 1980.

Vigness, David M. "The Lower Rio Grande Valley, 1836–1846." Master's thesis, The University of Texas, Austin, 1948.

———. "The Republic of the Rio Grande: An Example of Separatism in Northern Mexico." Ph.D. Diss., University of Texas, 1951.

Villareal, Roberto M. "The Mexican-American Vaqueros of the Kenedy Ranch: A Social History." Master's thesis, Texas A&I University, 1972.

Webb, Walter Prescott. *The Great Plains.* New York: Grosset & Dunlap, 1931.

———. *The Texas Rangers: A Century of Frontier Defense.* 2d ed. Austin: University of Texas Press, 1991.

Wilhelm, Stephen R. *Cavalcade of Hooves and Horns.* San Antonio: Naylor Co., 1958.

Will, James. *Cow Country.* New York: Grosset & Dunlap, 1927.

Worrell, Dorothy Ostrom. "Rita Alderete de San Miguel Was Pioneer Mother and Eagle Pass Business Executive." *Eagle Pass Guide*, Centennial Edition, 1949.

Xavier, Sister Mary. *Father Jaillet: Saddlebag Priest of the Nueces.* Corpus Christi: Diocese of Corpus Christi, 1948.

Zapata County Historical Society. "Zapata County Folklore." Unpublished booklet in Zapata County Museum, 1983.